a short history of

~boston~

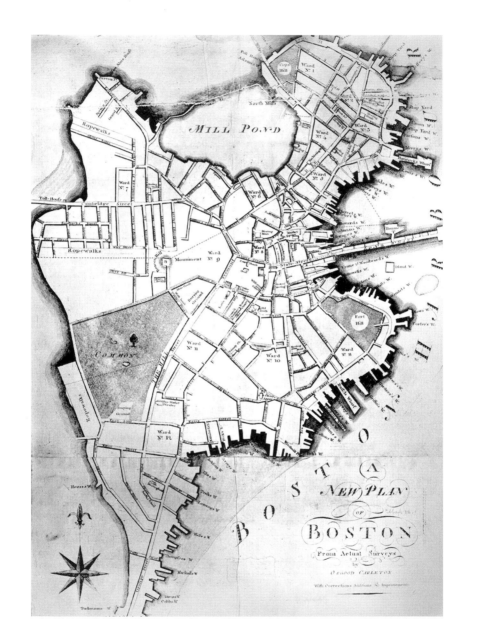

a short history of

boston

Robert J. Allison

COMMONWEALTH EDITIONS
BEVERLY, MASSSACHUSETTS

For Bernard Bailyn

Fourth Printing, April 2006

Library of Congress
Cataloging-in-Publication Data
Allison, Robert J.
A short history of Boston /
Robert J. Allison.
p. cm.
Includes index.
ISBN 1-889833-47-9 (pbk.)
1. Boston (Mass.)—History. I. Title.
F73.3.A45 2004
974.4'6—dc22   2003023069

Front cover image: "Southeast View of
the Great Town of Boston" (1700s),
courtesy of The Bostonian Society/Old
State House. For all other illustration
credits, see page 128.

Printed in Canada.

Cover and interior design by
Laura McFadden Design, Inc.
laura.mcfadden@rcn.com

Published by Commonwealth Editions
an imprint of Memoirs Unlimited, Inc.
266 Cabot Street, Beverly, MA 01915
www.commonwealtheditions.com

contents

view from long wharf

FROM THE END OF LONG WHARF, YOU CAN SEE TEN thousand years of history.

On the islands of the harbor, created by the glaciers that shaped New England's coast, the Massachusett people fished and farmed. They called this harbor Quonehassit, and it gave them oysters, clams, cod, and occasionally a whale.

Across these waters the English began to come in the 1620s, trading with the Massachusett and others, and then opening their own trade with the rest of the world.

The English built Long Wharf and the town of Boston around it. When the town's people resisted laws passed by the British to govern them, troops landed on Long Wharf to enforce the law, and on March 17, 1776, the British forces sailed from Long Wharf, leaving Bostonians to govern themselves. The city of Boston, its gleaming towers and crowded neighborhoods, is the result of successful trade and revolution. To the airport across the harbor still come thousands of immigrants to make new lives in the New World.

Quonehassit today is a different world from the one the Massachusett called home. The land has changed, and the harbor has changed. For three centuries the people of Boston dumped their garbage in it, and by the 1950s it was an open sewer. But today, thanks to a massive cleanup, it is one of the world's cleanest harbors. Like the Massachusett who stood on its marshy shores, you might see a porpoise or a seal breaking its surface. ⌐

1

from quonehassit to boston

BEFORE THE ENGLISH ARRIVED, the Massachusett lived on the islands in the summers, fishing in the harbor and building elaborate fish weirs, nets that trapped fish swept in at high tide. Excavations in the Back Bay in the early twentieth century uncovered a weir more than an acre in size. More recent archaeological work on Spectacle Island has uncovered shell middens, tremendous piles of clamshells left over hundreds of years by the Massachusett. In the winter, the Massachusett retired up the Neponset River to the Blue Hills, or up the Charles and Mystic Rivers to the north

Boston in 1630. This view of the Trimount from Charlestown was painted on the side of
a fire engine in the 1830s.

and west (their name, Massachusett, means "people of the great
hills"). They hunted deer and other animals. They grew corn, beans,
squash, and tobacco, trading with the Wampanoag and Pequot to the south
and west, the Nipmuck and Abenaki to the north. When English, French,
and Dutch traders began to arrive, they traded with them as well.

Sometime between 1617 and 1619, a ship from Europe brought a devastating plague to the Massachusett. Entire villages disappeared. There may
have been three thousand native people living along the Massachusetts
coast in 1616; three years later, barely five hundred remained alive.
Chicatabot, leader of the community along the Neponset, survived the
plague. His neighbor to the north, Nanepashemet of the Mystic, died.
Nanepashemet's widow survived to lead the survivors in their devastated
land. The name she called herself is unknown, but history records her as
the "Squaw Sachem."

In 1624 Samuel Maverick built a trading post at Noddle's Island, almost
directly across the harbor from where you stand at the end of Long Wharf.
Maverick traded with the surviving Massachusett and others for furs and
corn, which he then traded to fishermen and others venturing into the

Fish weir at high tide

area, including the English who started a colony at Plymouth in 1620. By 1626 Maverick had a new neighbor, William Blackstone, a minister in the Church of England. Blackstone had come to the New World as the chaplain of an attempted colony at Wessagusset, which later became Weymouth. When the expedition failed, Blackstone decided to stay in the New World. He left Weymouth for Quonehassit and built his house across the harbor from Maverick, on the peninsula the Massachusett people called "place of clear waters," or Shawmut, for its fine fresh spring water. Maverick and Blackstone, Nanepashemet and Chicatabot—all lived peacefully along the shores of Quonehassit.

IN 1630, A LARGER GROUP OF EUROPEANS arrived along the marshy shores of Quonehassit. John Winthrop, an English lawyer, along with several hundred followers of the Puritan way, left England to found a religious commonwealth—a community sharing in a common endeavor—in the New World. They believed England had grown corrupt and decadent, and the Church of England, despite having broken with the Roman Catholic Church a century earlier, still maintained too many of its rituals and traditions. Winthrop and his followers wanted to form their own individual relationships with God, doing so as members of a community of saints.

In April 1630 the expedition of more than a thousand men, women, and children gathered in Southampton, England. The Reverend John Cotton, one of the leading Puritan ministers of the day, preached a farewell sermon to the multitude. They sailed off with a charter authorizing them, as the Massachusetts Bay Company, to plant a colony somewhere between the Merrimack and the Neponset Rivers. Before making landfall, Winthrop presented his vision for this community in a sermon made on the flagship *Arbella*, "Christian Charitee: A New Modell Hereof." Quoting the Bible, Winthrop said that "wee must Consider that wee shall be as a Citty upon a Hill, the eies of all people are upon us." Having the whole world watching made the consequences of failure drastic: If they failed, "wee shall be made a story and a by word through the world, wee shall open the mouthes of enemies to speake evill of the wayes of god and all professours for Gods sake . . . , and cause theire prayers to be turned into Cursses upon us till wee be consumed out of the good land whether wee are goeing."

How would they avoid this ruin, which Winthrop, after two months on the rough Atlantic, called a "shipwreck"? The men and women of the colony must form one community, "follow the Counsell of Micah, to doe Justly, to love mercy, to walke humbly with our God," to be "knitt together in this worke as one man, . . . abridge ourselves of our superfluities, for the supply of others necessities," to make each others joys and sorrows our own, "rejoyce together, mourne together, labour and suffer together," in the "unitie of the spirit in the bond of peace."

After landing at Naumkeag (now Salem), where most of the original settlers had already died, Winthrop set out to find a more congenial place for his colony. He ventured south and, in Quonehassit, found what he was looking for. He met with Blackstone and with Maverick, and at Mishawum found remnants of a great house, built by the Naumkeag expedition, which he converted into a dwelling. The others followed, and by the end of summer nearly a thousand people crowded into this new settlement. They changed the name of Mishawum to Charlestown, for the king, and the site of this first settlement today is City Square and Paul Revere Park.

Charlestown had not enough water and too many mosquitoes. An old friend of Blackstone's was in the Winthrop party, and the Shawmut recluse invited some of Winthrop's band to join him on the healthier Shawmut peninsula. Blackstone was soon overwhelmed by the Puritans. He decided that having left England to get away from the Lords Bishops, he did not like the Lords Brethren any better, and he retired further into the continent, building a new home along a Rhode Island river (now named for him). Maverick stayed on Noddle's Island, both a friend and a rival to Winthrop and the Puritans, trading with the native people and entertaining more exuberantly than the Puritans approved. As with Blackstone, who gave his name to a river, Maverick left his name behind. Maverick Square in East Boston is roughly the site of his Noddle's Island home; one descendant

William Blackstone. Sculptor Thomas Ball, best known for his equestrian statue of George Washington in the Boston Public Garden, made this model for a statue in his Florence studio in 1884.

John Winthrop

OCCUPATION: Lawyer, governor of Massachusetts

LIFETIME: 1588–1649

FAMILY: Born in England. Married four times: Mary Forth, 1605 (died 1615); Thomasina Clopton, 1615 (died 1616); Margaret, 1618 (died 1647); Martha,1647. Sixteen children.

ACCOMPLISHMENTS: Governor of Massachusetts Bay Company, 1629–1630. Governor of Massachusetts Bay Colony, 1631–1633, 1637–1639, 1642–1643, 1645–1649.

GREATEST CONTROVERSY: Presided over inquiry into Anne Hutchinson's heresy and ordered her banished.

John Winthrop

"[F]or wee must Consider that wee shall be as a Citty upon a Hill, the eies of all people are upon us, soe that if wee shall deale falsely with our god in this worke wee have undertaken and soe cause him to withdrawe his present help from us, wee shall be made a story and a by word through the world. . . ."

died in the Boston Massacre, and another ventured out to Texas, where he chose not to brand his cattle, which marked them as not belonging to anyone else. *Maverick* still means one who does not fall in with the established orthodoxy, whether of cattle or religious doctrine.

WINTHROP NAMED THE SETTLEMENT BOSTON, for the English town from which many had come. Standing on the end of Long Wharf, looking back toward the city, one can imagine the settlement by looking left, to the towers on East India Wharf, just past the Aquarium. The shoreline curved inward, to the fleck of gold on top of the Old State House, in a straight line up Long Wharf and State Street, and from that point curved outward again, to the right, toward the granite blocks of Commercial Wharf. Atlantic Avenue marks approximately the boundary between the tidal flats, which were marshy ground at low tide, and the deeper waters of the harbor. Dock Square, in front of Faneuil Hall, became the settlement's center. Buildings spread to the northeast, along the shore of what became the North End, and to the southeast, in what then was the South End.

Beyond the settlement to the west rose the three peaks of the Trimount. The eastern peak was named Mount Cotton, for clergyman John Cotton, who built his house on it after arriving in the mid-1630s; the center peak was Beacon Hill, the tallest point on the peninsula, from which a beacon could be shone warning of attacks or other calamities; the westernmost was called Mount Whoredom for the illicit activities taking place on its slopes. Today Mounts Cotton and Whoredom are leveled, their ground used to fill the Mill Pond and Charles Street, respectively, and Beacon Hill itself is reduced and smoothed. The name *Trimount* lives on in Tremont Street, which runs from the foot of Beacon Street along Boston Common and into the South End.

The settlement's heart was along the water, and the colonists spread along the rivers feeding Quonehassit. Winthrop believed that these rivers, the Mystic and Charles to the north and the Neponset to the south, led far

In the Tercentenary Monument on Boston Common, William Blackstone greets John Winthrop. Here, the model for Blackstone was James Michael Curley.

into the rich interior, perhaps even to the mythical "Lake of the Iroquois" to the northwest, which supposedly teemed with beavers, whose pelts were valued in Europe for making felt hats. Unfortunately the rivers reach no further inland than Dedham and Medford. Disappointed in not finding hordes of beaver pelts, Winthrop and his followers found other ways to survive.

The colonists learned to fish, raise cattle and hogs, cut down timber, and build ships. The Massachusetts Bay Colony thrived by combining all of these activities, building barrels to pack their salted codfish, pork, and beef, and loading these goods onto ships to trade in Barbados and Jamaica. On those West Indian islands, African slaves produced sugar. The Massachusetts ships brought salted meat and codfish to feed the slave laborers, taking in return molasses. The molasses was brought back to Boston, refined either into sugar or rum, and then shipped to Europe or to Africa, to be traded for manufactured goods or for more slaves for the West Indies. Massachusetts thrived not so much through producing codfish and ships as through selling goods in this trans-Atlantic trade. Edward Randolph noted in 1676 that "Boston may be esteemed the mart town of the West Indies."

This trade in cattle and lumber with the West Indies made trade with the Indians for corn and furs less important. Some English had hoped to convert Native Americans to Christianity—in fact, the colony's original seal shows an Indian saying, "Come over and help us." Winthrop had made peace with the Squaw Sachem and with Chicatabot (who died of smallpox in 1631), and the colony had founded Harvard College in 1636, in part to educate Native Americans to be ministers. But by the end of the first decade, the Massachusetts Bay settlers were pushing out the original Massachusett people, as well as natives on the periphery. In 1637, the Massachusetts colony went to war against the Pequots of Connecticut, massacring hundreds and bringing others back to Boston, where they were sold as slaves to the British colonies in the West Indies.

In the wake of this, John Eliot, a minister from the First Church in Roxbury, set out to evangelize among the Indians. Dressing and living simply, Eliot learned the Massachusett language and traveled throughout Massachusetts preaching to the native people. Believing that the Massachusett, Wampanoag, and Narragansett could not become Christian unless they also lived like the English, Eliot established "praying towns" for his converts, beginning with Natick in 1651. He translated the Bible into the Natick dialect, and in 1663 published this translation, the first Bible to

View from Charlestown in the 1830s, two hundred years after the view shown on page 9. It was painted on the other side of the fire engine.

be printed in the New World. Eliot established more than thirty praying towns by 1674, when there were about a thousand Christian Indians in Massachusetts Bay and Plymouth. Still, the conversion of Indians owed perhaps as much to the threat of invasion as it did to Eliot's moral appeal.

As the colony spread over the Shawmut peninsula and up the rivers that fed into the harbor, it prospered. Its prosperity, though, was not what Winthrop had intended. His vision was for a community held together as one person, but quickly he saw how difficult this vision was to sustain. By the late 1630s, his leadership, and the leadership of Boston's established clergy, was under challenge from a number of independent thinkers. One, Anne Hutchinson, a devout Puritan influenced by John Cotton's teachings, found the other ministers' sermons uninspiring. After Sunday services she met with other parishioners to discuss the Bible readings and lessons.

Soon, large groups gathered every week in Hutchinson's home, and the Puritan hierarchy became alarmed. She was summoned to a hearing before Winthrop, Cotton, and the other ministers and magistrates. What gave her the right or the power to teach the Gospel? She insisted that she was performing her religious duty by discussing scripture with others. When, under questioning, she finally said that God spoke directly to her, she was charged with heresy and banished from the colony. Hutchinson went first to Rhode Island, founded by another Puritan dissident, Roger Williams, and then to Pelham Bay in the Dutch colony of New Amsterdam. There she and her children were killed by Indians, in what is now New York City's Pelham Park along the Hutchinson River. Hutchinson's legacy lived on,

Anne Hutchinson

OCCUPATION: Midwife

LIFETIME: 1591–1643

FAMILY: Born in England, daughter of an English minister. Married merchant William Hutchinson, 1612 (died 1642). Eleven children.

ACCOMPLISHMENTS: Led weekly meetings to read Scripture in her home, attended by up to eighty people. After banishment from Massachusetts, founded Portsmouth, Rhode Island. Following husband's death, moved with five youngest children to Pelham Bay in Dutch colony of New Amsterdam, where she and four children were killed by Mahican Indians.

Anne Hutchinson statue, Massachusetts State House

GREATEST CONTROVERSY: Charged with heresy for her unlicensed preaching. Excommunicated and exiled by General Court.

At end of heresy trial: *"You have power over my body but the Lord Jesus hath power over my body and soul; and assure yourselves thus much, you do as much as in you lies to put the Lord Jesus Christ from you, and if you go on in this course you begin, you will bring a curse upon you and your posterity, and the mouth of the Lord hath spoken it."*

however. Her friend Mary Dyer returned to Boston to spread the spiritual message of Quakerism—and was executed as a heretic.

DESPITE RELIGIOUS TENSION AND ETHNIC CONFLICT, Boston grew. Dock Square remained the commercial center of the settlement, but along the waterfront to the north and south stretched wharves and docks. The North End was a crowded waterfront neighborhood, home to some of the colony's wealthiest merchants as well as to its most desperate poor and the many in between. Along the waterfront, on Ann Street, were taverns and boarding houses catering to sailors and dockworkers. Farther up the hills were the homes of the merchants and ministers. Where the gleaming towers of Boston's financial district now stand was the South End, a less crowded neighborhood dominated then by Fort Hill, the last line of defense for the town in case of invasion. Fort Hill was leveled after the Civil War and used to fill in the South End waterfront. Between Fort Hill and Dock Square were ropewalks and wharves; between Fort Hill and the Common were the garden homes of Boston's elite; and along the shoreline to the south, stretching toward Boston Neck, were more wharves and taverns.

Boston's economic success masked its feelings of insecurity. While merchants were trading throughout the Atlantic world, the town was threatened by the French and their Indian allies to the north, by the Dutch, and even by the British government. In the 1670s the Massachusetts colony went to war against the Wampanoags and other Indian peoples. Metacom, or King Philip, the leader of the Wampanoags, mobilized Indians throughout New England in a war against the English. But Philip could not win the support of the Mohawks to the west, and though the Indians destroyed four dozen New England towns, the war was devastating to the Indians. The fearful colonists in Boston, unable to find Philip, instead attacked their own allies, the praying Indians of Natick and other communities John Eliot had

Mary Dyer statue, Massachusetts State House

founded. These Christian Indians were incarcerated on Deer Island and Long Island in Boston Harbor, many dying before they were finally released. Other Indians were less fortunate and from the harbor islands were shipped off to slavery in the West Indies.

At the end of the seventeenth century, the British government began to see the importance of its colonies. This meant closer attention from London, which did not please the Bostonians. King James II in the late 1680s tried to consolidate Massachusetts with the other New England colonies into the Dominion of New England, which would be governed from New York. Edmund Andros, New York's royal governor, would now also govern New England. Andros angered the Puritan hierarchy when he declared his intention to build an Episcopal church, King's Chapel, on a portion of the Old Burying Ground on Tremont Street.

The Bostonians arrested Governor Andros as a usurper and sent minister Increase Mather to England to plead their case. Fortunately for them, Parliament deposed King James in what the British called the Glorious Revolution. In his place, Parliament installed Queen Mary, a Protestant daughter of James II, and her husband, Prince William of the Netherlands. Thanks to Increase Mather's lobbying, William and Mary granted a new charter to the Massachusetts Bay Colony, guaranteeing some self-government but making the governor a royal, rather than a local, appointee.

Boston's old Feather Store, Dock Square, on the left, built in the 1680s. This scene was the subject of countless Boston photos and sketches before the Feather Store's demolition in the 1860s. Faneuil Hall is in the background.

ALL THESE TROUBLES AND TRAGEDIES — Indian warfare, religious tension, the loss of the charter—were signs to the devout colonists that Satan was at work. They fully expected a more visible sign of Satan's work, and it came in the summer of 1688. Martha Goodwin, a thirteen-year-old girl in Boston's South End, accused the family's laundress of stealing. The laundress's mother, Goodwife Glover, an Irish Catholic widow who spoke only Gaelic, retorted harshly to young Martha, who was suddenly "visited with strange fits." Martha and her younger brother suddenly had sharp pains in their necks and hands, and were struck "Deaf, sometimes Dumb, and sometimes Blind." Their tongues one moment were forced down their throats, the next nearly pulled from their mouths; they barked like dogs, crawled on all fours, and suffered excruciating pain from imaginary knives.

"Come over and help us": The 1629 seal of the colony of Massachusetts was used until 1684.

Doctors could not help the children. But the Reverend Cotton Mather, son of Increase, took Martha into his home to pray with her and study her bizarre symptoms. Mather described Goody Glover as an "ignorant and scandalous old Woman," whose late husband had "complained of her, that she was undoubtedly a Witch."

Metacom, or King Philip, whose uprising against the Puritans terrorized New England

Goody Glover confessed to bewitching the children, and after her arrest the tormented children had a brief rest. But when one of Goody's relatives encountered the children and "entertain'ed them with her Blessing, that is, Railing," the fits resumed.

Goody Glover confessed to being a witch, though she could not answer questions except in Gaelic. She could repeat the Lord's Prayer in Latin, but not in English, and when she was sentenced to die she proclaimed that the children's suffering would not end with her death because others were also

Cotton Mather

OCCUPATION: Pastor, Second Church of Boston

LIFETIME: 1663–1728

FAMILY: Born in Boston, son of Increase Mather and grandson of ministers Richard Mather and John Cotton. Married three times: Abigail Phillips (died 1702); Elizabeth Clark Hubbard (died 1713); Lydia Lee George, who became mentally unstable. All but six of fifteen children died in childhood.

Cotton Mather

ACCOMPLISHMENTS: Author of more than four hundred books, including the first history of New England, *Magnalia Christi Americana.* Elected Fellow of the Royal Society of London.

GREATEST CONTROVERSIES: Supported the witchcraft trials in 1692. Was nearly assassinated in 1721 for advocating smallpox inoculation.

When young Benjamin Franklin whacked his head on a beam after visiting, Mather advised him, "Stoop! Stoop! You are young, and have the world before you; Stoop as you go through it, and you will miss many hard thumps."

in a league with her and her "Prince" and "spirits." Though Goody Glover was hanged on Boston Common, the Goodwin children continued to suffer. Young Martha, in Mather's home, spent days in motion as though riding a horse and could not bear to have the ministers pray with her. Finally, after a day of fasting and prayer, the fits eased.

Cotton Mather recorded the story of the Goodwin children's affliction in a book, *Memorable Providences, Relating to Witchcrafts and Possessions* (1689). Three years later, when young women in Salem began experiencing similar symptoms, Mather's book provided the background necessary to understand what was at work. During the Salem outbreak, nineteen alleged witches were executed and hundreds were accused of leaguing with the Devil.

⌐ ⌐ ⌐

COTTON MATHER HAD A LIFELONG INTEREST in good and evil and in the workings of the invisible world. While Mather was a devout Christian, seeing the hand of God in all creation, he kept informed about the latest scientific advances and contributed his own observations to the world of science. In 1713 he was elected a Fellow of the Royal Society of London, the leading scientific organization of the day. When smallpox struck Boston in 1721, Mather advocated inoculation—taking a bit of pus from a person with a mild case of the disease and injecting it into a healthy person, who then developed a mild case of smallpox but who survived with lifelong immunity—as a way to prevent the epidemic. Mather learned of inoculation from two sources. His slave Onesimus, a Coramantee from West Africa, told Mather that his people practiced inoculation; and in the *Transactions* of the Royal Society, Mather read about inoculation practiced in Turkey.

But to many in Boston, Mather's advocacy was more than enough to show inoculation to be a bad thing. Ministers like Mather had brought on the persecution of the Quakers in 1658, and Mather himself was behind the hanging of suspected witches in 1692. Now, in 1721, he proposed inoculation, or "self-procuring the Small Pox." As hundreds of Bostonians died excruciating deaths from smallpox, the debate raged over inoculation and over the role of Cotton Mather in this and other catastrophes.

Printer James Franklin launched his own newspaper, the *Courant,* to combat inoculation. Franklin's attacks on inoculation turned into attacks on the colony's leadership, so much so that authorities suppressed his paper in the early 1720s. Banned from publishing, Franklin technically put the paper into the hands of his younger brother and apprentice, Benjamin, though James continued to run the show. Benjamin began publishing his own series of essays lampooning the colony's elite and using the pseudonym "Silence Dogood," a mocking reference to Cotton Mather.

Benjamin Franklin, son of a Boston soap-maker and his Quaker wife, could not get along with his older brother and wound up leaving Boston for Philadelphia while still a teenager. Though he began his long career as a printer and writer by mocking Cotton Mather, Franklin also was deeply influenced by the older man. Mather's 1711 essay, "Bonifacius," or "To do

THE BIRTH-PLACE OF FRANKLIN,
WHICH STOOD IN MILK STREET, OPPOSITE THE OLD SOUTH CHURCH, BOSTON.

LEFT: Birthplace of Benjamin Franklin, Milk Street. RIGHT: Boston's first public statue, dedicated in 1856 to honor Franklin, who had run away as a teenager more than a century earlier. The front panel shows Franklin at work in the print shop.

good," made a deep impression on young Franklin. "I have always set a greater value on the character of a doer of good, than on any other kind of reputation," Franklin wrote in his own *Autobiography* half a century after Mather's death. And, Franklin said, if he had indeed been "a useful citizen, the Public owes the advantage of it to that book."

Only later in life did Franklin see Mather's profound influence. Franklin by then was in Philadelphia, where he modeled his own life on the "character of a doer of good." His vision of the involved citizen, actively engaged with creating a better world, owed much to the vision of Winthrop and Mather.

2

boston in the revolution

AT THE HEAD OF LONG WHARF IN 1657, the town built a central marketplace, thanks to the bequest of merchant Robert Keayne. Here on the ground floor country folk coming to town to sell their goods could dry off in rainy weather or warm up in cold weather. On the upper floor, the town elders could confer and the courts could sit. It burned in 1711 but quickly was replaced by a new brick town house, with a market on the ground floor and town and provincial offices and meeting rooms upstairs. This served as the seat of Massachusetts government from 1713 until 1796, and

Andrew Oliver, brother-in-law of Thomas Hutchinson, lieutenant governor, and briefly a stamp-tax agent

today, as the Old State House, it is the second oldest public building in the nation. The Town House stood at the center of Boston's commercial world, on Long Wharf. From the balcony of the Council Chamber, from where he read royal proclamations, the governor could watch ships preparing to carry the British flag to all parts of the world.

Here in 1748 Governor William Shirley was meeting with his council when they heard an angry mob outside surrounding the building. This crowd had marched up Long Wharf, escorting a detachment from the British warship *Preston*. These British sailors had been sent ashore to impress into the Royal Navy any able-bodied men they could find. The Royal Navy treated its sailors brutally and therefore found it difficult to enlist men, who were better paid, fed, and treated in the merchant service. Under British law, a naval commander could impress into service any British subject anywhere in the world.

The men and women in the Boston mob permitted the British officers to go inside and meet with the governor. But while Shirley met the press gang, he could hear the Bostonians outside demanding that he send the *Preston* and its press gang away. Shirley recognized that British warships might come and go, but he would have to live with the men and women outside. He sent the press gang away empty-handed. While British ships would impress sailors in other ports in the American colonies, none would ever again try to do so in Boston—despite the need for men to fight the Seven Years' War, which began in 1756.

After the Seven Years' War (called by Americans the French and Indian War) ended in 1763, the British government tried to raise revenue by taxing the American colonists. The Stamp Act of 1765 imposed a small tax on all printed documents. In Boston, Andrew Oliver signed on to sell the stamps. Little did he know that by agreeing to uphold the law of the empire, he would help trigger the empire's end in America. On the night of August 14, 1765, a mob descended on Oliver's Long Wharf office. Believing that Oliver was storing the stamps inside, the mob broke in and, not finding the stamps, tore down the shop and threw it into the harbor. A day later, Oliver was invited to visit the South End tavern where the mob's leader, Ebenezer Macintosh, a shoemaker, held court. Escorted by a group of citizens, Oliver arrived at the large elm in front of the tavern to see his own effigy hanging by its neck. Oliver was asked if he would like to continue as tax agent. Fearing that the mob would not be satisfied with simply hanging his effigy, Oliver resigned.

Oliver's brother-in-law, Lieutenant Governor Thomas Hutchinson, privately disapproved of the Stamp Act but publicly believed Parliament had power to tax the colonists. Privately he also believed Oliver should not have surrendered to the mob. But on August 26 a mob appeared at Hutchinson's home in the North End and, after forcing the lieutenant governor and his daughter to leave, ransacked the house, destroying Hutchinson's manuscripts (he was writing a history of Massachusetts) and cutting the eyes out of his portrait. Hutchinson did not resign but did move to his country house in Milton.

In Parliament, some wanted to punish the Bostonians for their destructive protests. Others sympathized. Isaac Barre, a member of Parliament, argued that the colonists were asserting their rights as Englishmen not to be taxed without their consent. The protestors were not lawless mobs, Barre insisted, but "the freeborn sons of liberty," seeking to preserve their liberties as English men and women. The term "Sons of Liberty" stuck, and the elm from which they hung Oliver's effigy became the Liberty Tree. As with the mob that blocked the *Preston* crew's attempt to impress

The Liberty Tree, where the Sons of Liberty gathered, at the corner of Essex and Orange (now Essex and Washington) Streets. The tree was cut down during British occupation.

Thomas Hutchinson

OCCUPATION: Merchant, historian, governor of Massachusetts

LIFETIME: 1711–1780

FAMILY: Born in Boston, great-great-grandson of Anne Hutchinson. Married Margaret Sanford, 1734 (died 1753). Five sons, two daughters.

ACCOMPLISHMENTS: With Benjamin Franklin, proposed a plan of union for the American colonies, 1754. Lieutenant governor of Massachusetts, 1758–1771; chief justice of Superior Court, 1760–1769; royal governor of Massachusetts, 1771–1774. Author, *History of the Province of Massachusetts Bay*. Received honorary Doctorate of Civil Laws, Oxford University, July 4, 1776.

GREATEST CONTROVERSIES: Supported idea that British Parliament could legislate for American colonies. Brother-in-law appointed a stamp tax agent; sons appointed tea merchants. Legalistic approach prevented him from averting Boston Tea Party. Spent final years in exile in England.

Thomas Hutchinson

"I know of no line that can be drawn between the supreme authority of Parliament and the total independence of the colonies. . . . Is there anything which we have more reason to dread than Independence? I hope it will never be our misfortune to know, by experience, the difference between the liberties of an English colonist, and those of the Spanish, French, or Dutch."

Bostonians, the Sons of Liberty resisted any attempt to establish an arbitrary, tyrannical government.

～ ～ ～

THESE ATTEMPTS CONTINUED, however. In 1767 Parliament, insisting it did have the power to tax all subjects of the British empire, created a new system of taxes. Knowing that collecting these taxes in Boston would be difficult, Governor Francis Bernard requested two regiments of troops, who arrived at Long Wharf in October 1768. The arrival of troops made a tense situation explosive.

Bernard had requested the troops, but their arrival was a problem. Where would he keep them? The leaders of the town, not wanting to have British regulars among them, thought Bernard should house his troops on Castle Island. But for Bernard, that would put his troops too far away to do any good. He wanted them to be based in the town itself. But where?

The town refused to provide space in any of the available public buildings, and private homes were out of the question. Winter was fast approaching, and although the troops could camp on the Common during the summer, winters in Boston were too cold for that kind of roughing it. Then Bernard found the perfect solution. Just off the Common stood the Manufactory House. Built fourteen years earlier to train poor people how

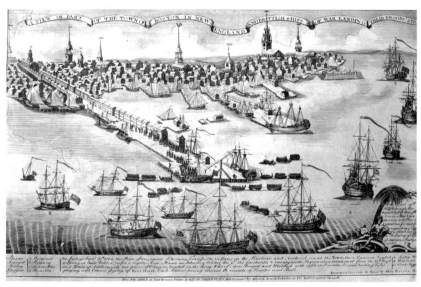

Arrival of the British troops, 1768. Paul Revere's engraving emphasizes the number of church steeples, suggesting that in this peaceful and God-fearing town, British troops were unnecessary to preserve order.

to weave cloth, the Manufactory House now was home to tenants, who paid very little in rent in return for the privilege of weaving on the basement looms. These tenants were powerless, not connected to the merchants or other leaders, and in no position to resist the governor's order to house troops among them.

Bernard sent Sheriff Stephen Greenleaf to seize the Manufactory House. Sheriff Greenleaf knocked on the door, and the tenants told him to leave. He insisted that he and a company of troops be allowed in. The tenants refused. The soldiers surrounded the building to starve out the tenants. To Greenleaf's surprise, the townspeople surrounded the soldiers, lobbing loaves of bread through the windows to feed the besieged inmates. Then Greenleaf noticed a basement window and decided to take possession of the Manufactory House from inside. He and some soldiers climbed through the window, only to find themselves trapped in the basement.

For two weeks, the Manufactory House was the site of this tense stand-off—soldiers surrounding the building, townsfolk surrounding the soldiers, the sheriff and soldiers prisoners in the basement, the tenants prisoners in their own residence. Governor Bernard saw that seizing the Manufactory House would not work, and so called off his siege. This was the first time American colonists resisted armed British troops, and though there was some minimal bloodshed, the colonists were successful. They resisted; the British troops backed down. Bernard had to rent quarters for his troops, and the Massachusetts Assembly began pushing to have the governor recalled.

The soldiers arrived as the town struggled through a postwar recession. Business had boomed during the war, but now Boston struggled. Matters were not helped by the new taxes Parliament imposed, nor by town leaders like Samuel Adams calling for a boycott of British goods to protest those taxes. By early 1770, trade was stalled, and some merchants hoped either to evade the taxes by smuggling or simply to accept the taxes and sell British goods.

Ebenezer Richardson, a merchant, saw nothing wrong with the British government taxing American trade. Richardson had ways of finding out which American merchants were evading their duties to the Crown and informing the customs agents of which ships and shops to search. By upholding the law of England, Richardson was violating the unwritten law emerging in Boston. In February, when word spread that a Boston merchant was defying the boycott and selling British goods, a mob descended on the merchant's shop. Richardson went to the merchant's aid, helping

Samuel Adams

OCCUPATION: Political leader, governor of Massachusetts

LIFETIME: 1722–1803

FAMILY: Born in Boston, son of a prosperous merchant, Samuel Adams Sr. Married Elizabeth Rolfe, 1749 (died 1757 after delivering stillborn son). Six children, only two of whom survived infancy. Married Elizabeth Wells in 1764.

ACCOMPLISHMENTS:
Helped organize American Revolution. As clerk of Massachusetts Assembly, organized the Committee of Correspondence to keep union between colonies; organized similar connections between towns of Massachusetts; directed opposition to Stamp Act and other revenue laws as violations of Massachusetts Charter; organized public funerals and propaganda campaign in wake of Boston Massacre; organized Boston Tea Party; organized Continental Congress and signed Declaration of Independence. Governor of Massachusetts, 1794–1797.

GREATEST CONTROVERSIES:
A failure as a businessman, Adams devoted all his energies to political agitation. Blamed by Thomas Hutchinson for the Revolution. Was the only American exempted from King George III's offer of amnesty to rebels if they reconciled themselves to the British crown, though it is unlikely he would have accepted amnesty if offered.

Samuel Adams, pointing to the Massachusetts Charter, in a painting by John Singleton Copley

"We are reduced to this dilemma, either to sit quiet under this and every other burden that our enemies shall see fit to lay upon us as good-natured slaves, or rise and resist this and every other plan laid for our destruction, as becomes wise freemen."

him barricade his home and shop against the angry crowd. From inside the house, a gun fired into the crowd, and across the street eleven-year-old Christopher Seider (sometimes spelled *Sneider* or *Snider*) fell dead. The crowd dispersed in shock. Samuel Adams had the boy's body taken to Faneuil Hall, and Richardson was charged with murder. Richardson was convicted but later pardoned. On the last day of February, Adams organized the largest public funeral the American colonies had ever seen. Wrote the celebrated black poet Phillis Wheatley,

> *Snider behold with what Majestic Love*
> *The Illustrious retinue begins to move*
> *With Secret rage fair freedom's foes beneath*
> *See in thy corse ev'n Majesty in Death.*

Two thousand people moved by majestic love followed the boy's body from Faneuil Hall, where his funeral was held, past the Town House, where the governor and council met, down to the Liberty Tree, and then up to the Common to Seider's grave in the Granary.

The funeral rubbed raw the nerves of Bostonians and British authority, which was now dressed in the uniforms of the Fourteenth and Twenty-ninth Regiments. Many of these men, poorly paid Irish Catholics, had brought their wives and children along and now were competing for jobs and housing with Bostonians at the bottom of the town's economic ladder. All of these factors—religious, economic, and political—made it impossible that the soldiers could fulfill their mission of preventing disorder in the tense town. These tensions erupted on March 5, 1770, when an angry mob surrounded a company of British troops outside the Town House. The soldiers opened fire; four men fell dead and seven were wounded (one of whom died the following week).

Samuel Adams saw this as an inevitable consequence of using armed troops to enforce the law in a community and demanded that the troops be removed. They were sent to Castle Island. Adams organized a public funeral for the victims, all of them mourned together at Faneuil Hall. From Faneuil Hall ten thousand mourners followed the four caskets through the narrow streets, south past the Town House where they had fallen, past the rope walk where the first fight had taken place, to the Liberty Tree on Boston Neck, around the Liberty Tree and up to the Common, along the Common, and past the Manufactory House to the Granary Burying Ground, where the four men were buried next to

Christopher Seider. Thirty-three years later, Samuel Adams would be buried beside them.

Artist Henry Pelham painted the riot scene, calling it *The Fruits of Arbitrary Power*, and coppersmith Paul Revere made an engraving of the massacre on King Street. As the soldiers awaited trial, the town of Boston sent Revere's drawing and its own report on the event to England, demanding that the troops be removed farther away than Castle Island. Samuel Adams's cousin John defended the soldiers, who were tried for murder, and all but two were acquitted. Those two were branded on their thumbs. All the troops left Boston in 1771.

BOSTON REMAINED QUIET UNTIL 1773. That year several seemingly unrelated events converged to renew the conflict. Thomas Hutchinson, who had become governor when Bernard was recalled, wanted the Assembly to meet in Cambridge, beyond Boston's influence. The Assembly, under the leader-

The Boston Massacre, 1770. Paul Revere's engraving of the massacre scene was sent to England and throughout the colonies to inflame public opinion against British authority.

John Adams, painted by Benjamin Blyth. Adams successfully defended the British soldiers accused in the Boston Massacre. If the men had been executed, he said later, it "would have been as foul a Stain upon this Country as the Executions of the Quakers or Witches."

ship of its clerk, Samuel Adams, began moving to recall Hutchinson, just as they had forced Governor Bernard out four years earlier.

Halfway across the globe, the British East India Company had bankrupted itself in conquering India. To ease the company's distress, Parliament had given it a monopoly on all the tea sold in the British empire. Parliament also designated the merchants in each port who would be permitted to sell the tea. In Boston, two of the three designated merchants were Thomas Hutchinson's sons, Elisha and Thomas Jr.

When the *Dartmouth* docked at Griffin's Wharf in November, the Sons of Liberty quickly surrounded it, keeping the tea from being unloaded. Samuel Adams organized mass meetings, first in Faneuil Hall and then in the Old South Meeting House, to protest the arbitrary power Parliament exercised.

Finally, on December 16, 1773, about one hundred men dressed as Mohawk Indians streamed out of taverns and Masonic meetings along the South End waterfront, and within an hour had dumped all of the tea into the harbor. More than £9,000 sterling (worth more than $1.2 million today) was destroyed, in what became known as "the destruction of the tea" and later "the Boston Tea Party." In other port cities the locals either impounded the tea or forced it to be sent back to England.

When Parliament heard what had happened, it closed Boston Harbor, suspended the Massachusetts government, and sent General Thomas Gage, commander in chief of British forces in North America, to govern the rebellious province. Parliament hoped to isolate Boston and Massachusetts and was certain the other colonies would fall into line. But Samuel Adams, behind-the-scenes leader of the Boston town meeting and clerk of the Massachusetts Assembly, had already prepared a network: a Boston Committee of Correspondence to communicate with other Massachusetts towns and a Committee of Correspondence in the Assembly to communicate with other colonies. By the time the British government shut down Massachusetts' commerce and government, Adams had created a network throughout the other colonies that he hoped would come to his province's support.

In London, the Massachusetts Assembly had its own agent, Benjamin Franklin, to make its case. Franklin had done well since fleeing Boston. By the age of forty-two he was so successful as a printer that he could devote himself to science and politics. Now he was living in London, a Fellow of the Royal Society, lobbyist for Massachusetts as well as Pennsylvania, New Jersey, and Georgia, and the most famous American of his time. He was postmaster for all the American colonies, and his son was the royal governor of New Jersey. Months before the destruction of the tea, Franklin had requested that the king's Privy Council hear the Assembly's charges against Thomas Hutchinson.

Unluckily for Franklin, the Privy Council hearing happened just two days after London learned that the tea had been destroyed. Franklin came to the Privy Council wearing a new suit of Manchester velvet. The chamber was packed with the curious and angry, in no mood to hear complaints from Bostonians. For two hours Franklin stood silently while the British solicitor general attacked him—as a self-interested office-seeker, as a schemer and traitor, as a man without honor. Anger at the loss of the tea turned into anger at Franklin, and the hearing on Hutchinson turned into a humiliation of Franklin. Franklin had come to the hearing hoping it

The destruction of the tea, December 16, 1773

could help save the Empire; he left believing the Empire was not worth saving. The suit he had bought with such high hopes he put away; he wore it only twice more: in 1778, when he signed the treaty between France and the United States, and in 1783, when he signed the treaty with Britain recognizing American independence.

∼ ∼ ∼

IN SEPTEMBER 1774, Samuel and John Adams, along with John Hancock, set out for Philadelphia for the first meeting of a Continental Congress. For the Adamses, the big question was, would the other colonies support Massachusetts? Or would they follow Parliament in seeing Massachusetts as a particularly troubling place, one whipped into a frenzy by Adams and other radical leaders? While the Congress hoped to reconcile the colonies with the Empire, the Congress also was determined to support Massachusetts in her extremity. After all, the delegates reasoned, if Parliament could suspend the Massachusetts government and close Boston Harbor, it could also suspend their governments and close their ports.

Henry Bacon's *General Gage and the Boston Boys,* depicting boys who complained that the British camp on the Common interfered with their sledding

As General Gage and his troops occupied the town of Boston, a new government—or actually the old government—emerged in the rest of the province. People in the towns continued to elect their own magistrates, tax collectors, and delegates to the Assembly, even as Gage declared that only he could appoint local officials and that the Assembly had no business meeting at all. By early 1775, two governments operated in Massachusetts. Officially, Gage was the governor, but his power extended only to the areas controlled by his troops. In the rest of the province, voters at town meeting appointed local committees of safety to govern the towns and also sent delegates to a provincial Congress to govern Massachusetts. Men and women in Massachusetts who remained loyal to the British Crown found they had to leave their homes for Boston to put themselves under Gage's protection, while Bostonians whose loyalty remained with their home province fled from the town. Boston's population shrank from about fifteen thousand to fewer than five thousand, and Gage and his troops found themselves prisoners in the town they occupied.

Gage had his forces seize gunpowder held in Cambridge (now Powder House Square in Somerville) in September 1774. Trying to disarm the rebels, Gage instead aroused the countryside into fear of military attack. When he tried to seize more munitions stockpiled in Concord in April 1775, Gage's forces encountered armed militia. The British troops fired on the Lexington militia, who dispersed. The British marched on to Concord, where the militia from the entire surrounding area had now assembled to prevent further British advance. The militia at Concord stood their ground and chased the British forces back to Boston. From throughout New England, militia forces now swarmed into Cambridge and Roxbury to keep the British in Boston.

Gage tried to break out of Boston in June 1775. He planned to cross over to Charlestown and, with his troops, sweep around into Cambridge, dispersing the militia camped there, and then to Roxbury to clear out the militia gathered there. The night before Gage attacked, the militia fortified Breed's Hill. The Americans had been sent to fortify Bunker Hill, the larger peak, but the commander decided Breed's Hill made a better line of

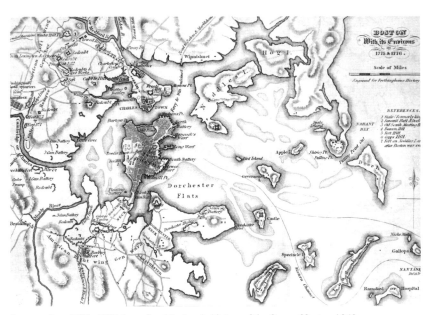

Boston, circa 1775–1776, from Frothingham's *History of the Siege of Boston*, 1849

defense. An error by a British mapmaker has forever misnamed the battle as the Battle of Bunker Hill, not Breed's Hill.

To save ammunition and make sure their shots hit their mark, the American commander Colonel William Prescott ordered, "Don't shoot 'til you see the whites of their eyes." The American militia waited until Gage's troops had reached the summit before opening fire. At close range the shots devastated the British, who retreated to the bottom. There they regrouped and tried again. Again they reached the summit but were turned back. As the well-trained, well-drilled, and well-supplied British troops advanced a third time, the Americans, on the summit of Breed's Hill, were running low on ammunition. The men in the fortifications held their ground long enough to allow most of their forces to retreat.

At the end of the day, the British held the hill, but nearly nine hundred of their troops lay dead on the slope, and the American forces had retreated safely to Cambridge. It was a tactical victory for the British but a moral victory for the Americans—they had held off the best-trained army in the world. "I wish we could sell them another hill at the same price we did Bunkers Hill," General Nathanael Greene wrote. Two weeks after this battle, George Washington arrived in Cambridge to take command of the American forces.

THIS WAS WASHINGTON's second visit to the Boston area. Nearly twenty years earlier, in late February and early March 1756, Washington had come to have Governor William Shirley, the supreme commander of military forces in North America, resolve a dispute over seniority at a frontier outpost in Maryland. While waiting for Shirley to confirm that he, as colonel of the Virginia forces, outranked a captain in the Maryland forces, Washington had time to lose four pounds at cards, buy new clothes, and admire Governor Shirley's country estate in Roxbury. Washington was so taken with the house that when he had an opportunity to build his own estate at Mount Vernon he copied some of the architectural details. (Now known as the Shirley-Eustis

The home of Governor William Shirley in Roxbury, now known as the Shirley-Eustis House. Downtown Boston is to the left.

William Shirley

OCCUPATION: Lawyer, general, governor of Massachusetts, governor of the Bahamas

LIFETIME: 1694–1771

FAMILY: Born in England. With wife, Lady Frances Barker (died 1746), moved to Boston to practice law, 1731. Nine children; two oldest sons died in Seven Years' War, oldest daughter died in childbirth, younger son succeeded Shirley as governor of Bahamas. On diplomatic mission to France in 1751 married Julie, daughter of his French landlord, although she did not come to America. Retired to his Roxbury estate with his daughter, Elizabeth Hutchinson.

ACCOMPLISHMENTS: Royal governor of Massachusetts, 1741–1749; 1753–1756. Organized successful attack on French stronghold at Louisbourg, 1745. Commander of British forces in North America in early years of Seven Years' War. Appointed governor of the Bahamas, 1761–1767.

GREATEST CONTROVERSY:
Sent to coordinate British attacks on French fortifications on Niagara, 1755, but was stymied by New York colony's resistance to his military authority and strategy. Relieved of command.

Governor William Shirley

On learning of Boston's representatives to General Court, 1771, John Hancock, Thomas Cushing, Samuel Adams, and John Adams: "Hancock I know, and Cushing I know, but where the devil this brace of Adamses came from I cannot say."

House, it is the only remaining colonial governor's palace in the nation. The house at Williamsburg is a reproduction.)

But Washington had not come to Cambridge in 1775 to shop or gamble or study architecture. He had two military objectives. One was to mold the men assembled in Cambridge and Roxbury into a fighting force. The other was to use this force to liberate Boston. From Rhode Island, where she had fled with other patriots, Phillis Wheatley wrote an ode to the new hero:

> *Proceed, great chief, with virtue on thy side,*
> *Thy ev'ry action let the goddess guide.*
> *A crown, a mansion, and a throne that shine,*
> *With gold unfading, WASHINGTON! be thine.*

Before he could pursue the crown, mansion, or throne, Washington had to force Gage out of Boston. He had more fortifications built on the hills surrounding the town. In the early winter months of 1776, Henry Knox, formerly a Boston bookseller, brought to Cambridge fifty-nine cannon captured at Fort Ticonderoga on Lake Champlain. Knox and eighty teams of oxen had pulled the cannon 300 miles on sleds across Vermont, New York, and Massachusetts. Washington placed the cannon at strategic points, but he still did not have command of the town, the fleet, or the fort at Castle Island. He ordered the batteries at Cambridge to open fire on the town, diverting the British into thinking the attack would come from the north. Meanwhile Washington had batteries built on Dorchester Neck, now South Boston. On the night of March 3, the cannon were quietly taken through Roxbury to Dorchester Neck and placed on these strategic heights overlooking Boston, the harbor, and Castle Island. Washington had surrounded the British.

Osgood Carleton's map of Boston, 1775

Phillis Wheatley

OCCUPATION: Poet

LIFETIME: 1753–1784

FAMILY: Born in Africa. Married John Peters in 1778. Three children, none of whom survived infancy.

ACCOMPLISHMENTS: Although brought to Boston as a slave, learned to read and write. In 1773 published *Poems, on Various Subjects, Religious and Moral,* in London and Boston, first poetry book published by an African American. Poetic talents noted by John Hancock, Thomas Hutchinson, George Washington, and British society in general.

GREATEST CHALLENGES: Became free on death of owner, 1778. In general economic hard times could not publish another book of poetry. Died in poverty.

Phillis Wheatley

"I, young in life, by seeming cruel fate
Was snatch'd from Afric's fancy'd
* happy seat:*
What pangs excruciating must molest,
What sorrows labour in my
* parent's breast?*
Steel'd was that soul and by
* no misery mov'd*
That from a father seiz'd his babe
* belov'd:*
Such, such my case. And can I then
* but pray*
Others may never feel tyrannic sway?"

ABOVE: Castle Island fortifications after the British evacuation

BELOW: Dorchester Heights today, in a watercolor by South Boston artist Dan McCole. The 1902 monument commemorates Washington's placement of cannons here to force the British evacuation of Boston.

On March 17, 1776, General Gage realized he could no longer hold Boston. His troops marched to Long Wharf, boarded the British fleet, and sailed away. Never again would hostile troops march in the town of Boston. General Washington led his own troops into the town by way of Boston Neck, and townspeople who had evacuated during the occupation began streaming back. They found that fences, shutters, and furniture had been used for kindling, that the Liberty Tree had been chopped down, and that Faneuil Hall had been used as a barracks and the Old South Meeting House as a riding school. Boston slowly began to revive, and from the balcony of the Town House, where royal governors had proclaimed the king's will, on July 18, 1776, citizens—no longer subjects—gathered in King Street to hear the Declaration of Independence read. Shortly after this, King Street became State Street. When in 1789 Washington returned as president of the United States, the long road connecting Boston to Roxbury became Washington Street.

3

boston in the new nation

AFTER INDEPENDENCE, BRITAIN no longer protected American commerce. British ports in the West Indies, once the most lucrative ports for Boston, now were closed to American trade. In the Mediterranean, Britain encouraged Algiers to attack American ships. With their two main outlets shut off, Bostonians sought other markets. In 1787, a group of Boston investors sent the *Columbia* to China, carrying a load of ginseng. It returned with a cargo of tea. This trade had its financial origins in Boston, but the trade quickly became one between China and the Pacific Northwest, with furs purchased from Indians along the Columbia River being sold in China for tea or silver. Ultimately the silver found its way to Boston, where the wealth of the China Trade created new fortunes. In Canton, China, Boston was thought to be a large and prosperous country of its own, and south of the Blue Hills the Indian village of Ponkapoag was renamed Canton in recognition of these new trading ventures.

In the 1790s, the Washington administration determined to protect American trade by building a navy. Edmund Hartt's North End shipyard began building USS *Constitution* in 1793. By the time the ship was launched four years later, the United States and Algiers had made peace, but France was now at war with the Americans. Shortly after the French war ended in 1800, Tripoli declared war on the United States. In response, *Constitution* sailed for the Mediterranean as flagship of the American forces under Captain Edward Preble and won peace from Tripoli in 1805. When the United States and England went to war in 1812, *Constitution* again sailed, this time under command of Isaac Hull. Hull encountered a British frigate, the *Guerriere,* southeast of Nova Scotia. The men in the British navy were experienced at war, having fought for nearly twenty years. In hundreds of engagements with enemy ships, the British had lost only five. But Hull and *Constitution* forced the *Guerriere* to surrender.

No one knows if he was American or British, but during the battle a sailor who saw British cannonballs bounce off *Constitution's* hull called out, "Huzza! Her sides are made of iron!" The ship's sides are actually made of wood—an outer layer of white oak and a frame of live oak, hardy wood from Georgia and Florida, which resists rot as well as cannonballs. Victorious *Constitution* returned to Boston with her prisoners and a new nickname—Old Ironsides.

Bostonians celebrated this victory, but one of the war's most crushing defeats happened just off Boston Light. In the

Boston Harbor, in needlepoint. Lydia Whithington completed this hand-crafted map at Mrs. Rowson's school in 1799.

USS *Constitution* ("Old Ironsides"), the world's oldest commissioned warship still afloat

twilight hours on the first of June 1813, Bostonians could hear the thunder of cannon as the frigate *Chesapeake* fought the British frigate *Shannon*. Captain James Lawrence was bold and daring, but his men were poorly trained, and many had spent their last night on shore celebrating. The *Shannon* systematically and effectively cut apart the *Chesapeake*, though Lawrence held his position until he was hit by a British shot. As he was carried below he gave a final order: "Don't give up the ship!" But without him the battle went badly. In the moments before he died, he was stunned to learn that his men had indeed given up the ship. Vessel, crew, and Captain Lawrence's body were taken to Halifax, where the British honored his valor with a hero's funeral before returning his body to Salem (and finally to New York). Though the *Chesapeake*'s timbers now frame an English mill, Lawrence's final words remain the motto of the U.S. Navy.

BY THE TIME THE WAR ENDED IN 1815, Boston merchants had found new outlets for their capital. American commerce had all but stopped during the embargo of 1808, during the tense years before the war, and during the war itself. Merchants saw a need to diversify their holdings and did so by investing in manufacturing. A group of Boston merchants, the Boston Associates, began planning the first large-scale manufacturing plants in the nation.

At Waltham, the Boston Associates built a factory to make cloth, using the water of the Charles River to power the looms. The Waltham experiment was notable for bringing under one roof all aspects of wool manufacture—combing and carding to make the fibers straight, spinning the yarn, and the final weaving of cloth. This became a model for future American manufactures. Previously, individual farmers would shear sheep, and their wives would spin the yarn and weave the cloth. All of this happened in farmhouses throughout New England. Now the production would take place in factories, like the ones built at Waltham. In the 1820s, the Boston Associates bought land on the Merrimack River in Chelmsford, where they founded the town of Lowell, named for Boston's Lowell family. Connected by canal and later by railroad to Boston, Lowell produced cotton textiles.

Beacon Hill under excavation. Fifty feet were removed from the top between 1807 and 1832.

Both the raw cotton, brought from the southern states, and the finished cloth flowed through the port of Boston.

The newly wealthy Boston merchants wanted to escape the close confines of the North and South Ends, where they were surrounded by longshoremen and dockworkers, boarding houses and taverns. A group of investors, the Mount Vernon Proprietors, planned to develop Beacon Hill as a district of mansions. Its southern slope, facing the Common, would be the town's most prestigious area. The development faced two major obstacles. First, much of it was owned privately, and second, it was too steep to develop.

The Proprietors first set out to buy the land. One of the owners, portrait artist John Singleton Copley, had remained loyal to the British crown and now lived in London. The Proprietors approached him there. They did not tell him that they had plans to develop Beacon Hill or that they were already building a new State House not far from his pastureland. He sold them the land thinking it worthless pastureland, not knowing their grand plan to turn it into Boston's premier real-estate development.

Having bought the land, the Proprietors next made it suitable for building. Workmen carted the dirt in handcarts down the slope to the Mill Pond, filling in that basin. Architect Charles Bulfinch, designer of the new State House on Beacon Hill as well as many of the mansions of the Proprietors, laid out streets on the new land of the Mill Pond in a triangular pattern, creating an industrial barrier, the Bulfinch Triangle, between the new Beacon Hill neighborhood and the old North End.

᭞ ᭞ ᭞

Charles Bulfinch

OCCUPATION: Architect

LIFETIME: 1763–1844

FAMILY: Born in Boston. Married cousin, Hannah Apthorp, 1788. Eleven children.

ACCOMPLISHMENTS: Designed Massachusetts State House, 1796, and state houses in Connecticut and Maine. Designed first Boston theater as well as churches, public buildings, and houses throughout New England. Chaired Boston's board of selectmen, 1799–1817, overseeing police force and public works projects such as filling in of Mill Pond and turning Boston Common into a park. Became architect of U.S. Capitol and oversaw completion of central portion, 1817–1830.

GREATEST CONTROVERSIES: During building of State House, went bankrupt in attempt to build elegant Tontine Crescent on Franklin Street. While superintendent of police and chair of selectmen in 1811, was jailed one month for debt.

Charles Bulfinch

"My estimate of the cost of the state house was made many years since. . . . [M]y own experience since that time has convinced me of the fallacy of estimates in general, and especially in buildings of a public nature."

AS THE CITY WAS BUILDING ANEW, it also tried to hold onto the past. In 1791 a group of Bostonians formed the Massachusetts Historical Society, the first organization in the United States dedicated to preserving history. The Massachusetts Historical Society is still one of the nation's premier

Ice being loaded on Tudor Wharf for shipment to the tropics. Frederic Tudor sent his first 130 tons of ice to the West Indies in August 1805, and the ice business made Tudor Wharf one of the city's busiest places.

repositories of historical records and artifacts. Not only does it house the voluminous papers of the Adams family, but it also has the largest collection of Thomas Jefferson's papers outside the Library of Congress, a cast of Abraham Lincoln's hands and face and the pen he used to sign the Emancipation Proclamation, the weathervane from the old Province House, the papers of aviation pioneer Godfrey Lowell Cabot, and over 115,000 photographs, along with newspapers, prints, sculptures, Phillis Wheatley's writing desk, and a jar of tea preserved from the Boston Tea Party.

In 1806 a group of Boston intellectuals, led by minister William Emerson, formed the Anthology Club, which was devoted to literature, history, and the arts. The Anthology Club also began collecting books and paintings, outgrowing various meeting places before building the Boston Athenaeum in 1849 on Beacon Hill. These cultural institutions suggest that the tumultuous port city of the 1760s had become a more refined place in the nineteenth century. A loyalist who returned to Boston in 1808 noted, "The great number of new and elegant buildings which have been erected in this Town, within the last ten years, strike the eye with astonishment, and prove the rapid manner in which the people have been acquiring wealth." Bostonians found new goods to trade in China and India—in the 1830s Frederic Tudor built a fortune shipping ice to the Caribbean, India, and China—and Boston became a center for trade in goods and in ideas. Bostonians were both holding onto their past and vigorously creating a future.

No man better demonstrates the way Bostonians reshaped their world than Ralph Waldo Emerson. Son of the Reverend William Emerson, Ralph was born in Boston in 1803. After graduating from Boston Latin and from Harvard, he taught school in Boston and Roxbury. (Schoolmaster Hill in Franklin Park recalls Emerson's stint as a teacher there.) His brief career as a Unitarian minister began in 1829 at Boston's Second Church and ended after the death of his first wife in 1831. After this he pursued life as a philosopher, calling on Americans to renounce the tired models of Europe and to transcend their mundane and empty lives by embracing new individualistic values. Emerson's Concord neighbor, Henry David Thoreau, put the ideas of transcendentalism into practice during a year spent on Walden Pond. His winter tranquility at Walden was interrupted, he noted, by "one hundred Irishmen, with Yankee overseers, come from Cambridge every day to get out the ice" for Frederic Tudor to ship around the world. Thoreau imagined sweltering people along the Ganges being cooled by Walden's ice.

Boston's international trade owed much to the ingenuity and technical skill of men like Donald McKay. From his East Boston shipyard, McKay and his workmen launched some of the fastest sailing vessels ever built. McKay's ships—the *Flying Cloud*, *Great Republic*, and *Sovereign of the Seas*—were designed for both speed and cargo, to carry goods from Boston to California around Cape Horn and to bring back gold from California to Boston. But the very nature of the clipper's success—the fact that Bostonians were perfecting clipper ships when steam power was rendering sails obsolete—ultimately prevented Boston's further advance. New York, with canals linking the city to the interior, ultimately became the nation's financial capital.

At his East Boston shipyard, Donald McKay built the fastest clipper ships ever to sail, including the *Flying Cloud* (shown here in a painting by Henry A. Lachance).

Elizabeth Palmer Peabody

OCCUPATION: Educator

LIFETIME: 1804–1894

FAMILY: Born in Billerica, Massachusetts. Never married. Introduced her sisters Sophia and Mary to future husbands, Nathaniel Hawthorne and Horace Mann.

ACCOMPLISHMENTS: Founded first kindergarten in United States, 1860. Wrote histories and books on transcendentalism and educational theory. Operated book store on West Street. Published transcendentalist journal *The Dial* and other works on back-room press.

Elizabeth Palmer Peabody

"I cannot understand unhappy people. . . . Those people who say that life is not worth living, find it so because they do not go to work to make it worth living. Why does sadness overpower them?"

While Emerson's ideas were the intellectual center of Boston's culture and commercial prowess made its culture flourish, the Peabody sisters were its social center. Elizabeth Palmer Peabody opened a school for girls in Boston in 1822 when she was eighteen. In her spare time, she studied Greek at the girls' school being taught by a teenaged Ralph Waldo Emerson. A lifelong teacher and educational advocate, Peabody later started the first kindergarten, based on a German concept, in the United States. She introduced her sisters to the men they would later marry: Sophia to novelist Nathaniel Hawthorne, and Mary to political leader and education advocate Horace Mann. Elizabeth Peabody's bookshop on West Street became the hub for a stellar intellectual circle, and on her printing press she published three of Hawthorne's novels and the transcendentalist journal, *The Dial*, edited by Margaret Fuller and Emerson. Peabody wrote two articles about the transcendentalist Brook Farm community of West Roxbury, which her brother-in-law Hawthorne later used as the basis for *The Blithedale Romance*.

⌒ ⌒ ⌒

BOSTON WAS BECOMING the center of an american culture, though not all cultural forms flourished. The Puritans had forbidden theater, and any kind of drama was banned until 1793 (though to get around the ban some entrepreneurs advertised "moral lectures," which in one case included tightrope dancing). Although Charles Bulfinch designed Boston's first theater in 1793, another was not built until 1827, and even then actors and playwrights found Boston a tough community. English actress, playwright, and novelist Susan Haswell Rowson settled in Boston in the decades after the Revolution. Though her novel *Charlotte Temple* was one of the bestsellers of the 1790s and she was one of the era's celebrated actresses, she needed to open a school for young ladies to support herself and family. Another beautiful young actress, Elizabeth Arnold Poe, gave birth

ABOVE: Young Ralph Waldo Emerson

BELOW: Horace Mann, educational reformer, abolitionist, and president of the State Senate

to a son in a Boston boardinghouse in 1809. After her death two years later, her infant, Edgar Allan Poe, was reared by relatives in Virginia. As an adult,

Poe had a lifelong contempt for the town of his birth. He regarded its people as shallow, smug, and self-satisfied, and its cultural attainments as minor. He nicknamed the town of his birth Frogpondia for the frog pond at the Common's center, a small and shallow pool whose puffed-up inhabitants croaked loudly about their accomplishments. ⌒

English actress, novelist, playwright, and schoolteacher Susannah Haswell Rowson, who settled in Boston after the Revolution

4

boston in the nineteenth century

WHEN BRITISH NOVELIST CHARLES DICKENS VISITED Boston in 1842, he was not interested in emerging transcendentalist ideas or in the relics of the colonial or Revolutionary past. He came to Massachusetts to see the factories at Lowell; he came to Boston to see Laura Bridgman.

Laura Bridgman was thirteen when Dickens visited her. She had been completely blind and deaf since she was two. Born on a farm outside Hanover, New Hampshire, she was fortunate enough to survive the scarlet fever that killed her sister. But it left Laura nearly dead for

Boston, from City Point near Sea Street, 1830s

months and without sight or hearing for the rest of her life. For five years she stayed home at the farm, sitting in her chair by the fire, able to communicate only through taps on the head from her family. In 1837 Samuel Gridley Howe brought Laura to Boston. Howe had opened the Perkins School a decade earlier, in a Fort Hill mansion donated by Thomas Handasyd Perkins, a China merchant. Howe moved the school in 1839 to the former Mount Washington Hotel near Dorchester Heights in South Boston.

Here Dickens saw Laura Bridgman, who had been taught to read and write. When Laura discovered that the symbols she had been feeling with her fingers and the patterns her teacher's fingers made in her hand had meanings, "at once her countenance lighted up with a human expression; it was no longer a dog or a parrot,—it was an immortal spirit, eagerly seizing upon a new link of union with other spirits!" Howe wrote that he "could almost fix upon the moment when this truth dawned upon her mind, and spread its light to her countenance." Laura Bridgman was the first deaf and blind person to learn language and to be able to communicate freely with others. The Massachusetts legislature, in addition to subsidizing the Perkins School, applauded Howe for this "grand achievement of science and patient beneficence," giving Bridgman and other afflicted people the "key of language" and "freedom instead of bondage, light for darkness." The work of the Perkins School earned an international reputation for Boston, and Dickens believed that Bridgman, the "sightless, earless, voiceless child," could teach the "self-elected saints with gloomy brows" lessons in charity and sympathy.

Laura Bridgman. The deaf and blind girl from Hanover, New Hampshire, teaches the deaf and blind Oliver Caswell to read.

BOSTON NEEDED LESSONS in charity and sympathy. The city was expanding rapidly and becoming an industrial and transportation center. Immigrants—Catholics from Ireland and Jews from Germany—were coming to the city in greater numbers. Boston's Protestants were not always welcoming. Small communities of Catholics and Jews had been tolerated in Boston since colonial times. Moses Michael Hayes, a Jew, started Boston's first marine insurance company in 1784, and later he became grand master of the Masonic Lodge. But Jews did not have a synagogue until 1843, and they could not even be buried in Massachusetts before 1844, when the first Jewish cemetery was created in East Boston.

The Perkins School's most famous students, Helen Keller (left) and Anne Sullivan. When Keller's parents in Alabama learned of the school's success with Laura Bridgman, they asked for a teacher for their daughter. Sullivan went to Alabama and later brought Keller back to South Boston.

An exceptional French Catholic priest, Jean de Cheverus, had enlisted Protestant support in building an elegant church, Holy Cross (designed by Bulfinch) on Franklin Street. Cheverus returned to France in 1825 (he became cardinal in Bordeaux) and left to his successor, Bishop Benedict Fenwick, a growing Irish Catholic flock.

Boston's immigrants crowded into the neighborhoods abandoned by the wealthier Bostonians, who had moved to Beacon Hill. The Irish immigrants arriving in greater numbers in the 1830s, and in a torrent in the 1840s, met hostility, not so much from the wealthier Bostonians who hired them as from the working-class Bostonians with whom they competed for jobs. Two savage riots in 1834 and 1837 were a result.

Bishop Fenwick oversaw the creation of Catholic schools because the public schools relied heavily on the Protestant Bible for instruction. And many wealthy Protestants, who were moving away from Calvinism toward Unitarianism, saw the Catholic schools as an alternative to the dogmatic Protestantism of the public schools. The Ursuline sisters had established a school on Mount Benedict in Charlestown (it is now in Somerville) where girls from Boston and Cambridge received an education.

Minister Lyman Beecher, a fiery evangelist and teacher who had moved to Ohio in the early 1830s, came back to Boston in 1834. In a series of sermons, he denounced what he perceived as a growing Catholic menace to American institutions. In the wake of his call for action against a Catholic threat, and owing to a rumor that one of the Ursuline sisters had fled from the Charlestown convent, a mob surrounded Mount Benedict in August 1834. As the sisters were waking their sixty

Cathedral of the Holy Cross, designed by Bulfinch, on Franklin Street in the 1850s. In the background is the spire of the Federal Street Church where Massachusetts ratified the U.S. Constitution in 1788.

LEFT: Archbishop Jean de Cheverus, Boston's first Catholic bishop, from a painting by Roxbury artist Gilbert Stuart. RIGHT: Bishop Benedict Fenwick, the first American-born leader of Boston's Roman Catholics

Immigrants arriving at Boston's Constitution Wharf, 1857, at the height of anti-immigrant bias

students and ushering them out the back door, the mob at the front started to set the convent on fire. The mother superior warned them that Bishop Fenwick had "twenty thousand Irishmen at his command in Boston," but Fenwick tried to avoid confrontation by dispatching priests to prevent Catholic retaliation. Protestant mobs, not satisfied with burning the convent, then tried to set fire to a Catholic church and burned the shanty homes of thirty-five Irish laborers.

In the wake of the fire, Protestant leaders tried to tone down the rhetoric. Members of the mob were brought to trial but acquitted, and the state refused to compensate the church for its losses. The Ursuline sisters relocated to West Roxbury, leaving the charred ruins on Mount Benedict as a monument to Protestant intolerance. Over the next decade, as tens of thousands of Irish immigrants came into Boston, the threat of ethnic violence lay barely concealed.

Violence came to the surface again in 1837. This time a group of working-class Boston firefighters disrupted a Catholic funeral procession on Broad Street. The firefighters and the Irish mourners began to brawl, and quickly two mobs, Catholic and Protestant, were battling all over the South End. The Irish barricaded themselves on top of Fort Hill, holding off swarms of Protestants trying to force them out. In the wake of the Broad Street riot, Boston's city officials reformed the Boston Fire Department, the oldest in the nation (founded in 1678), making it less a collection of social clubs and more a full-time professional force.

WHILE THE ARRIVAL OF IRISH CATHOLIC IMMIGRANTS was transforming the city, other Bostonians were beginning to memorialize the Revolutionary past. In Charlestown, the Bunker Hill Monument Association was attempting to build a suitable memorial to the Revolution. The association bought fifteen acres of land on Breed's Hill, site of the battle, and decided to build a 221-foot granite obelisk on its summit. On June 17, 1825, thousands of spectators watched a brilliant parade, its highlight more than one hundred surviving veterans of the battle marching up the hill—"Take your last look at us!" Elizabeth Peabody recalled one of them saying to the crowd—where Lafayette, accompanied by the Masonic lodge grand master, laid the cornerstone and then listened to association president Daniel Webster deliver an oration.

It was a grand day, but it would take eighteen years to finish the monument. Solomon Willard, the architect, first had to find granite. This he did in Quincy. Then, to get the granite from the quarries to the docks, he had to build a railroad—the first in the United States. The association ran out of money when the monument had reached a height of thirty-seven feet and had to sell off much of the battlefield to keep building. By 1839 the monument was eighty-two feet high, and the association again was broke. Its annual report in 1840 doubted that any living person would see the Bunker Hill Monument completed. But a group of women took over, hosting a fund-raising fair, and raised $30,000 to finish the monument.

On June 17, 1843, crowds again thronged to Charlestown, this time to dedicate the Bunker Hill Monument. President John Tyler and members of his cabinet came from Washington to hear Secretary of State Daniel Webster deliver another oration celebrating the monument's completion. Only thirteen Revolutionary veterans witnessed the dedication. Men and women who remembered the Revolution were scarce. Webster regretted that ill health prevented former President John Quincy Adams from attending the

Bunker Hill Monument in 1840, still unfinished after fifteen years of construction

John Quincy Adams refused to attend the Bunker Hill Monument's dedication because of Webster's "spouting" and President Tyler's expected attendance.

ceremony, as "whenever popular rights were to be asserted, an Adams was present" during the Revolutionary struggle.

In fact, Adams was not kept home by ill health but by disgust. In his diary the former president wrote that to see "John Tyler and his Cabinet of slave-drivers" desecrate the memory of Bunker Hill was more than he could stand. "Daniel Webster is a heartless traitor to the cause of human freedom," Adams wrote. "John Tyler is a slave-monger. What can these have to do with the Quincy granite pyramid on the brow of Bunker Hill?" He could not go to the ceremony for fear that he would burst with either moral indignation or laughter at the contrast between "the thundering cannons, which I heard, and the smoke of burning Charlestown, which I saw, on that awful day" in 1775 and the sight of "Daniel Webster spouting" and "John Tyler's nose with a shadow outstretching that of the monument."

IN THE MEANTIME, Boston had become the center of opposition to slavery. On Beacon Hill's north slope and in the North End lived a relatively small but important community of African Americans. In 1829 one of them, David Walker, a used clothing dealer with a shop on Brattle Street, published his *Appeal to the Colored Citizens of the World*. He called on slaves to resist their masters, pointing to the Declaration of Independence and the Bible as justification. Authorities in Savannah confiscated sixty copies brought in by a Boston sailor, and Georgia banned black sailors from taking shore leave. Mayor Josiah Quincy rejected appeals from Georgia and South Carolina to arrest Walker or confiscate his book. Walker's sudden death in June 1830 (some thought he had been poisoned) did not stop the black community in Boston from advocating an end to slavery.

Abolitionist
William Lloyd Garrison

William Lloyd Garrison, a printer from Newburyport, began publishing a newspaper

Josiah Quincy

OCCUPATION: Mayor of Boston, president of Harvard

LIFETIME: 1772–1864

FAMILY: Born in Boston, son of Revolutionary-era patriot Josiah Quincy Jr. Married Eliza Susan Morton of New York, 1794. Two sons and five daughters. Son and great-grandson, also named Josiah Quincy, served as mayors of Boston.

ACCOMPLISHMENTS: As Boston's second mayor (elected to five one-year terms, 1823–1829), built Quincy Market, eliminated gambling and prostitution in West End, reorganized fire department, established House of Correction and House of Industry (separating paupers from criminals), cleaned streets, and introduced new water and sewer systems. Later became president of Harvard. Wrote histories of Boston, the Boston Athenaeum, and Harvard and wrote biographies of John Quincy Adams and his father.

GREATEST CONTROVERSIES: As Federalist congressman, voted against the War of 1812. Opposed extension of slavery throughout career. As mayor, battled so long against entrenched interests he was defeated for reelection.

Mayor Josiah Quincy, in an engraving based on Gilbert Stuart's portrait. Faneuil Hall Marketplace, or Quincy Market, is in the background.

"Citizens of Boston! . . . Consider your blessings; consider your duties. . . . Let New England continue to be an example to the world of the blessings of free government, and of the means and capacity of man to maintain it. . . . In all times to come as in all times past, may Boston be among the foremost and the boldest to exemplify and uphold whatever constitutes the prosperity, the happiness, and the glory of New England."

Masthead from *The Liberator*, the abolitionist newspaper published by William Lloyd Garrison

called *The Liberator* in 1831, near the site of Walker's Brattle Street shop. Like Walker, Garrison saw the promise of American liberty as a sham when the American economy thrived through slavery. He saw the U.S. Constitution as a "covenant with death" because it allowed the sin of slavery to continue. With excerpts from Walker's *Appeal* and articles by other black writers, *The Liberator* became a paper for black and white abolitionists. Garrison advised abolitionists to boycott the political process rather than legitimize an unfair system by entering into politics.

Even though Boston had become the headquarters of the American antislavery movement, many Boston investors depended on slavery. Bales of cotton from the southern states came through Boston en route to Lowell. The Lowell mills turned the cotton into woven cloth, which was then shipped back south to clothe slave laborers. Beacon Hill incomes depended on this trade, as well as the trade in boots, shoes, ice, and granite being sent to the slave states. Daniel Webster and other "cotton Whigs" did not want to destroy the Union that made these incomes possible. Charles Sumner denounced this alliance between factory owners and slave owners, naming them the "lords of the loom and the lords of the lash."

The controversy even transcended the bounds of politics and economics. The nation's foremost scientist, Louis Agassiz of Harvard College, tried to justify slavery on the dubious ground that the races were fundamentally different. Agassiz, whose main area of expertise was glaciers and rock formations, tried to refute racial equality publicly and also tried to challenge Darwin's theories on evolution.

In March 1850 Webster committed a final outrage in the eyes of slavery opponents when he supported the Fugitive Slave Act. In an attempt to hold the Union together, congressmen from the North and South had to agree to certain compromises: California would enter the Union as a free, not

Louis Agassiz

OCCUPATION: Scientist

LIFETIME: 1807–1873

FAMILY: Born in Switzerland. Married Cecile Braun, 1833 (separated 1845; she died 1848). Three children. Married Elizabeth Cabot Cary, granddaughter of merchant Thomas Handasyd Perkins, 1850. Wife and daughters taught in Agassiz School in 1850s. After Agassiz's death, widow Elizabeth Agassiz founded and was first president of Radcliffe College, 1879–1903.

Louis Agassiz

ACCOMPLISHMENTS: Considered one of world's foremost scientists of nineteenth century. Pioneer in study of glaciers. Led collecting exhibitions to Amazon, Great Lakes Regions. Built Agassiz Museum at Harvard.

"A physical fact is as sacred as a moral principle. Our own nature demands from us this double allegiance."

GREATEST CONTROVERSY: Argued against equality of African Americans.

slave, state; slave trading would be restricted (but not eliminated) in Washington, D.C.; and slave owners could recover fugitive slaves, even in free states. Abolitionists wanted to see slavery abolished at all costs, but Webster thought the Fugitive Slave Act a necessary concession to southern states. As many as five hundred fugitive slaves may have been taking refuge in Boston at the time. But the Fugitive Slave Act extended slavery's power into Boston. Senator Robert Toombs of Georgia boasted that the law of

Massachusetts could not prevent him from calling the roll of his slaves on Bunker Hill. Within a month of the law's passing, more than one hundred slaves fled Boston for Canada, seeking freedom under the British flag. Boston's black community resolved to protect those who remained. In February 1851 a fugitive slave named Shadrach Minkins was apprehended and brought to a rendition hearing in Boston. Lewis Hayden, a fugitive from Kentucky now living on Beacon Hill, stormed the hearing with twenty men to rescue Shadrach from a return to slavery.

Hayden could not rescue Anthony Burns, a fugitive slave from Virginia claimed by his owner in 1854. Burns was taken to the Court House, where an angry mob tried unsuccessfully to free him, killing a federal marshal during their attempt. Burns was escorted by the mainly Irish Columbian Guards through silent crowds on State Street, the buildings draped in black bunting, the American flag hanging upside down across the street. The proprietor of Long Wharf refused to let the military force escorting Burns use the pier, so the procession turned onto T Wharf, where Burns was placed on a launch to carry him off to the steamer *John Tyler* for his return to slavery.

Burns returned to Boston less than a year later, his freedom purchased by the members of his Twelfth Baptist Church. But his return to

Editorial cartoon opposed to 1850's Fugitive Slave Law. William Lloyd Garrison is shown protecting fugitive slaves and Daniel Webster being ridden by the proslavery forces.

LEFT: Anthony Burns, 1855, surrounded by scenes from his life

ABOVE: The shackles that fugitive slave Burns wore when he was led back to slavery

slavery, more than any other event, turned Boston into an antislavery city. Even some former cotton Whigs came to see that the "conscience Whigs" had been right. As Abraham Lincoln would say a few years later, the Union could not survive half slave and half free; it must be either all free or all slave.

In 1854, slavery seemed to be taking over the Republic. In the Senate, Stephen A. Douglas proposed to allow slavery in federal territories if the people in those territories voted for it. As the Kansas territory was being organized, Samuel Gridley Howe and other Bostonians raised over $100,000 to send "Free-Soiler" immigrants into Kansas to keep it free. Free-Soilers in settlements such as Lawrence and Topeka fought slavery advocates so fiercely that the state was nicknamed "bleeding Kansas." Howe and five others formed the "Secret Six" with two specific goals: to finance John Brown's attacks on proslavery settlers in Kansas, and to arm Virginia slaves in a rebellion against slavery by seizing the federal arsenal at Harper's Ferry, Virginia. When John Brown called at their South Boston home, Julia Ward Howe recalled that he "looked like a Puritan of the Puritans, forceful, concentrated, and self-contained."

WHEN THE CIVIL WAR BEGAN in April 1861, Boston was transformed. "That's the death blow of slavery!" Samuel Gridley Howe announced when he heard that the South Carolina militia had attacked Fort Sumter in Charleston. Bostonians who had opposed abolition immediately took up arms when their country's flag was attacked. President Lincoln called for

Lewis Hayden

OCCUPATION: Clothing dealer

LIFETIME: 1811–1889

FAMILY: Born a slave in Kentucky. Escaped with wife Harriet, 1846. No surviving children.

ACCOMPLISHMENTS: Owned clothing store, second-largest black-owned enterprise in Boston. Home at 66 Phillips Street became abolitionist meeting place and station on Underground Railroad. Organized Boston Vigilance Committee to protect fugitive slaves; organized rescue of slave Shadrach Minkins, 1851; unsuccessfully tried to free Anthony Burns, 1854. Appointed messenger at State House, 1859. Persuaded John Andrew to run for governor, 1860. Elected to Massachusetts Legislature, 1872. Harriet left $5,000 to Harvard Medical School as scholarship to support black medical students.

GREATEST CHALLENGES: Mother driven insane by her owner. Once sold for a pair of horses. Arrested for role in rescue of Thomas Simms but acquitted when one juror refused to convict.

Lewis Hayden

"I have one child who is buried in Kentucky, and that grave is pleasant to think of. I've yet another that is sold nobody knows where, and that I can never bear to think of."

volunteers to put down the rebellion, and within three days Massachusetts sent three regiments to Washington. On April 19, the anniversary of the battles of Lexington and Concord, the Massachusetts troops had to fight their way through Baltimore, where pro-Confederate mobs controlled the city. The troops made it to Washington, the first to come to the capital's defense, but not without casualties.

Governor John Andrew, a Republican abolitionist who had hired lawyers to defend John Brown, had the bodies of the Massachusetts soldiers brought home to a funeral in King's Chapel. The war would not result in a quick triumph for the north; rather, it would call on sacrifices from all.

None could have predicted when the war began how thoroughly it would transform Boston and the nation. Among the first to volunteer were Boston's Irish, whose relations with the antislavery vanguard had been bleak. Now that the American flag had been fired upon, though, Irish and Irish American citizens flocked to enlist in the cause of the United States. Thomas Cass had commanded the Columbian Guards, who escorted Anthony Burns back to slavery in 1854. Now he led the thousnd men of the Ninth Regiment of Massachusetts Volunteers, who marched up Long Wharf on June 25, 1861, to receive their colors from Governor Andrew: "as Citizens of Massachusetts, assured that her honor will never be disgraced by the countrymen of Emmet and O'Connell." The Ninth fought at Bull Run, Antietam, Gettysburg, and the Wilderness. A month after the regiment had left Boston, it encamped outside Washington, on the slopes of Robert E. Lee's estate. Over breakfast the men talked with Lee's slaves. Company sergeant and historian Daniel Macnamara wrote that "in some unaccountable way" the Irish Ninth was "connected with their future destiny, and would in time lead them out of the house of bondage."

Leading the enslaved out of the house of bondage, though, was not yet Union policy. The regiment commanded by Colonel Fletcher Webster—Daniel Webster's son—had trained on Georges Island to a new song proclaiming that though "John Brown's body lies a'mouldering in the grave/His truth is marching on!" The men sang this song as they marched up State Street to receive their colors from Governor Andrew, conscious that they were retracing in reverse the route taken by Anthony Burns seven years earlier. The song quickly spread through other units until word came down from the U.S. Army command that the men were not to sing "John Brown's Body." The war was not to end slavery; it was to save the Union.

Thomas Cass

OCCUPATION:
Businessman, soldier

LIFETIME: 1822–1862

FAMILY: Born in Queen's County, Ireland; brought to Boston at nine months old. Married Adeline B. Cass. Four children.

ACCOMPLISHMENTS: Ran successful shipping company. Elected to Boston School Committee, 1860. Raised and trained all-Irish Massachusetts Ninth Regiment; commissioned as colonel, 1861; fought in Virginia, building Fort Cass near Falls Church. Died in Boston after being wounded at Malvern Hill, Virginia, July 1862.

GREATEST CONTROVERSY:
Commander in 1850s of all-Irish Columbian Guards, who escorted Anthony Burns back into slavery. Unit disbanded under orders of Know-Nothings, 1855.

Thomas Cass

After a Union battery mistakenly fired on a Union regiment, killing many, Cass was asked what his unit would have done if the battery had turned on them. "Done! I would have charged the battery, and by Heaven I'd have taken it, too!"

Whatever the official policy of the Union, the war was about slavery. In 1862 President Lincoln issued the Emancipation Proclamation and began allowing black men to enlist in the Union army. A recruiting station opened in the African Meeting House on Beacon Hill, and quickly free black men from Boston and from throughout the North formed the Massachusetts Fifty-fourth Regiment. Two of abolitionist Frederick Douglass's sons served in the regiment, which was led by white abolitionist Robert Gould Shaw and other white officers. The men trained in Readville (now Hyde

Park) before receiving their colors from Governor Andrew at the State House and marching down Long Wharf to steam to the war. The men of the Fifty-fourth, like the men of the Massachusetts Ninth, proved themselves in battle. Leading an assault on Fort Wagner on a sandy island off the South Carolina coast, they marched through a fiery artillery barrage to reach the gun emplacements of Fort Wagner. They broke through the Confederate defenses, getting to the tops of the barricades before the Confederates cut them down. Shaw died, and half of his men were either killed or wounded. Sergeant William Carney, the highest-ranking black non-commissioned officer (no blacks were commissioned), saw the flag bearer shot, but Carney snatched the banner before the colors fell. Folding the flag into his shirt, Carney crawled from the front lines to safety. "The old flag never touched the ground," he said later. The Fifty-fourth fought on, and Carney became the first African American to receive the Congressional Medal of Honor.

Men and women from Massachusetts made the war to save the Union into the war to end slavery. Samuel Gridley Howe traveled to Washington

Boston in 1859, showing the rail lines connecting the city to the rest of the world

1. Sergeant William Carney (1840–1908). A member of the Massachusetts Fifty-fourth Regiment, Carney is shown wearing the Congressional Medal of Honor he received in May 1900 for his actions at the siege of Fort Wagner, July 1863. After Carney died in an elevator accident at the State House, flags in Massachusetts flew at half-staff, the first time an ordinary citizen—an African American—was so honored.

2. Officers of heavy artillery at Fort Warren, Georges Island, 1864

3. Senator Charles Sumner celebrates the Emancipation Proclamation at Faneuil Hall. Louis Prang, a German immigrant in Roxbury, developed the process used to make this lithograph and later developed the first Christmas cards.

4. Julia Ward Howe (1819–1910), author, political activist, and widow of Samuel Gridley Howe, with her children and grandchildren. Best known for writing "The Battle Hymn of the Republic," she also established Mother's Day.

in the fall of 1861 to inspect sanitary conditions in the army camps. During the long train ride to Washington, Howe's wife, Julia Ward Howe, was struck by the sheer numbers of men in uniform encamped along the rail line, their numbers swelling as the Howes neared the capital. There men from throughout the Union, men of all ethnicities, encircled the city, drawn together in this cause. As her husband attended to his official duties—as one of the nation's best-known hospital managers, he had been summoned to head the U.S. Sanitary Commission—Julia Howe visited the camps of the Massachusetts men. She delivered her first public speech to the men of the First Massachusetts Heavy Artillery.

The Howes and Governor Andrew went to see a review of the troops in November, though the technical display was cancelled when the Confederate army cut off part of the Union force. Julia Howe's small group returned slowly to

Washington, their carriage moving alongside the soldiers who marched wearily back to camp. The Boston abolitionists began to sing. The soldiers cheered when they heard the forbidden strains of "John Brown's Body," calling out "Good for you!" and taking up the song.

Julia Howe woke up in the middle of the night. In her mind the strains of "John Brown's Body," the visions of the thousands of men in uniform marching to Washington, the flag-draped caskets in King's Chapel, and the struggle over slavery in Boston and now in Virginia kept her awake. She found a few sheets of her husband's Sanitary Commission stationery in the darkness of the hotel room, and certain that the nation was being transformed but not sure exactly how, she wrote:

> Mine eyes have seen the glory of the coming of the Lord.
> He is trampling out the vintage where the grapes of wrath are stored.
> He has loosed the fateful lightning of his terrible swift sword.
> His truth is marching on!
> Glory! Glory! Hallelujah! Glory! Glory! Hallelujah!
>   Glory! Glory! Hallelujah!
> His truth is marching on!

When she returned home to South Boston, Mrs. Howe sent a copy to James T. Fields, editor of the *Atlantic Monthly*. Fields paid her five dollars and printed the song on the first page of his February 1862 issue under the title "Battle Hymn of the Republic."

5

city transformed

THE CIVIL WAR TRANSFORMED the nation and, with it, Boston. African American residents and Irish immigrants were now part of the city's fabric. Boston's population had quadrupled since the 1820s and needed more space.

One of the boldest plans to expand the city grew out of one of the great failures of private enterprise, an attempt in the 1820s to use the Back Bay's surging tides to power mills along its shores. The Roxbury and Boston Mill Company built a Great Dam fifty feet wide from the edge of Boston Common across the Back Bay to Brookline. A Short Dam intersected the Great Dam at

Bird's-eye view of Boston in an 1850 engraving

Gravely Point, Roxbury. This created two basins. After the high tide filled the western basin, the water was forced into the larger receiving basin. This surge turned the wheels of eighty mills, grinding flour, sawing wood, spinning cotton or wool, rolling iron, and making anchors, cannon, farm tools, and grindstones. "How shall the citizens of Boston fill their empty stores?" a promotional brochure asked. "Erect these mills, and lower the price of bread."

At first, the possibilities seemed endless and so lucrative that one eager speculator tried to climb through the company's window to invest. The Back Bay's power did turn a few mills, but the Merrimack River, which other Boston investors had harnessed to turn the mills at Lowell and Lawrence, had more power. The Back Bay's industrial era was over. Railroad lines built across the receiving basin's marshy flats kept the area from flushing at high tide, and flushing is what the basin definitely needed. Sewer lines emptied from Beacon and Arlington Streets, next to what had become a dumping ground. Instead of a new industrial center, the Back Bay was a wasteland and public health menace. With conflicting lines of jurisdiction—some of the land belonged to Boston, some to Roxbury, some to the Commonwealth of Massachusetts—it was difficult to find a solution.

In 1856, the Commonwealth decided to fill its parts of the Back Bay, lay out new streets across the new land, and sell the building lots. The Great Dam from the Common to Brookline became Beacon Street, and the Short

Dam is now Hemenway Street. Trains brought gravel and stone from Needham, excavated by the new steam shovel invented by South Boston's John Souther, filling in the shoreline as far as Clarendon Street by the time of the Civil War and reaching Gloucester Street by 1871. By 1882 the entire Back Bay had been filled from the Public Garden to Kenmore Square. Wealthy Bostonians moved from Beacon Hill and the newly created South End to form a new social and cultural center. The land sales brought so much revenue that the Commonwealth could support new cultural institutions in the Back Bay, such as the Museum of Comparative Zoology (now the Museum of Science) and the Massachusetts Institute of Technology (now in Cambridge), and to endow other cultural institutions throughout the state.

At the center of this new showplace was Art Square, where the new Museum of Fine Arts opened on July 4, 1876. Drawing from the collections of the Boston Athenaeum and private collections of Boston families, the museum quickly acquired important works of nineteenth-century American art, as well as works from China, Japan, and India, and Egyptian and Greek antiquities. The museum also fostered new artists and encouraged scholarship and new trends in art. It opened a school in 1877 to help foster new artists and encourage scholarship and new trends in art. The museum, which moved to Huntington Avenue in 1909, has become one of the world's premiere cultural institutions.

In 1883, Art Square was renamed Copley Square, for the famous eighteenth-century portraitist. In 1895, the Boston Public Library (founded in

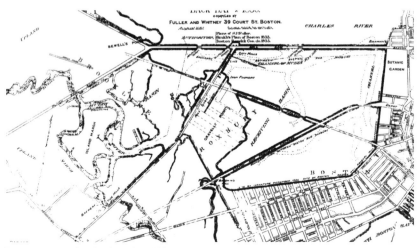

Proposed dams for the Back Bay, 1836

1849) moved there, to a building designed by Charles McKim and built of granite and Italian marble. It features artwork by John Singer Sargent, the French muralist Puvis de Chevannes, and Edwin Abbey, whose scenes of the quest for the Holy Grail use explanatory text by novelist Henry James. To reach out to a diverse population, the Boston Public Library created the nation's first branch library system, opening its first branch in East Boston in 1869.

ABOVE: Looking across the Back Bay from the top of the State House, 1854

BELOW: Loading gravel cars for the Back Bay. Trains operated around the clock to bring gravel from Needham to fill the Back Bay. To speed the work, engineer John Souther of South Boston invented the steam shovel, which would change landscapes around the world.

The creation of an art museum and a public library as the centers of the new Back Bay was a sign of Bostonians' community vision. In 1881 Major Henry Lee Higginson, successful businessman and Civil War veteran, called on Bostonians to create a symphony orchestra to provide "the best music at low prices, such as may be found in all the large European cities, or even in the smaller musical centres of Germany." No American city had such an orchestra, though Boston had been a musical center since earlier

Isabella Stewart Gardner

OCCUPATION: Art patron, museum founder

LIFETIME: 1840–1924

FAMILY: Born in New York City. Married Bostonian John Lowell Gardner Jr., 1860 (died 1898). Only son died as young child.

ACCOMPLISHMENTS: Built Venetian palace in Fenway (1903) and filled with artwork from Europe. Designated building and collection to be a public museum after her death.

GREATEST CONTROVERSY: Stood by German conductor Karl Muck when he was forced out of Boston Symphony during World War I.

Isabella Stewart Gardner, from Martin Mower's portrait, *Mrs. Gardner*

"Don't spoil a good story by telling the truth."

in the century. In 1833 the Boston Academy of Music had begun giving free music lessons to children and adults, and four years later it created a music program for Boston's public schools. The academy had shifted its focus to performing music in the 1840s, though it did not have a permanent professional ensemble. The New England Conservatory, founded in 1867, continues to bring young musicians to the city. Under Higginson's leadership, the Boston Symphony Orchestra became a model for other American orchestras, performing classical music for a broad audience (tickets sold out quickly) and offering lighter classical music at "Pops" concerts. In 1900 the Boston Symphony moved to its present home, at the intersection of Massachusetts and Huntington Avenues.

BACK ON THE OLD Shawmut Peninsula, the business district still crowded along Long Wharf, now State Street, and Dock Square. Just south of State Street rose Fort Hill, which had become a crowded urban slum. The wealthy merchant families who had made this area their home—Perkins, Wendells, Olivers—had fled to Beacon Hill, leaving their property to be rented out to immigrants. As Boston expanded across the Back Bay, planners also looked to make more land closer to the waterfront.

A Conversation in the Shadows at Trinity Place, a 1990s watercolor by Boston artist Dan McCole, shows the intimate space created in the city's center.

The city eyed the crowded tenement districts of Fort Hill and, in 1866, began clearing out the residents and leveling the hill, using the dirt to fill in Atlantic Avenue along the waterfront and the new South End and expanding Boston Neck.

The Catholic Church resisted the city's attempt to relocate its residents. The Church had moved its cathedral to the South End and had founded

Boston Public Library. Boston Herald-Traveler photographer Leslie Jones photographed the Boston Public Library in Copley Square, 1919.

Fort Hill in 1872. Removal of this crowded slum area began in 1866, to make room for a new business district

Boston College there in 1863. But the people in the crowded tenements of Fort Hill had faithfully worshipped in the granite Church of St. Vincent de Paul, bought from a fleeing Protestant congregation at the height of Irish immigration in 1848. The city wanted to seize the land on Fort Hill and demanded that St. Vincent's church be demolished. Most of the congregation now had moved to the lower end of South Boston, but they refused to let their old church be destroyed. They dismantled St. Vincent's stone by stone, loading the blocks onto barges and rebuilding it in their new neighborhood in April 1872.

St. Vincent's was fortunate to have moved to South Boston. A fire broke out on Summer Street, in central Boston, on the evening of November 9, 1872. By the next afternoon it had destroyed 770 buildings over sixty-five acres, from Summer Street to Milk Street, from Washington Street to the harbor. The Boston Fire Department's horses were just then crippled by equine flu, so help had to come from other towns and from as far away as Maine, New Hampshire, Rhode Island, and Connecticut. Miraculously, only thirteen people died in the inferno that destroyed the entire new business district: the offices of the *Transcript* and other newspapers on Washington Street, the wool warehouses on Franklin Street, the railroad station on Broad Street, the wharves, and Trinity and New Old South Churches, both of whose congregations were planning to move to the Back Bay. Old South Meeting House, the venerable site of the Tea Party protest meetings, was saved through valiant efforts of citizens and firefighters.

Boston rebuilt its commercial district and expanded by annexing Roxbury (1868), Dorchester (1870), and

Saving Old South Meeting House from the Great Fire, 1872

Charlestown (1873). Boston's Protestant civic leaders kept a tight grip on the city's financial and cultural resources from their homes in the Back Bay and Beacon Hill. The newly annexed neighborhoods—along with South Boston and East Boston and the crowded wards of the West and North Ends—were crowded with immigrants.

The old Protestant elite tried to shut the doors to economic power to these newcomers. Some immigrants found ways to advance through literature or the law, such as John Boyle O'Reilly, an Irish poet who edited *The Boston Pilot,* and Louis D. Brandeis, a Harvard-educated lawyer whose Jewish family had fled Germany after the 1848 rebellion.

Other immigrants found success through sports. John L.

ABOVE: Work crews on Franklin Street clearing rubble left by the Great Fire, 1872. Old South Meeting House rises in the background.

BELOW: The area destroyed by the Great Fire

John Boyle O'Reilly

OCCUPATION: Journalist

LIFETIME: 1844–1890

FAMILY: Born in Ireland. Married Mary Murphy of Charlestown, 1872. Four daughters.

ACCOMPLISHMENTS: Poet; owner and editor of the *Boston Pilot*.

GREATEST CONTROVERSIES: Court-martialed out of British army, 1866, after conviction for failing to report mutiny; death sentence commuted to twenty-three years in Australian penal institution. Escaped on American whaling ship and reached Boston in 1870.

John Boyle O'Reilly

"All that was good and beautiful in our dear native island, we should cherish forever. We have her faith and her honor to preserve and to make respected. We have sympathy with her trials and her efforts to be free. But we cannot, as honest men, band together in American politics under the shadow of an Irish flag."

Sullivan became one of the country's great athletic heroes by winning the heavyweight boxing championship in 1882. All New England mourned ten years later when he lost the heavyweight title—on the same day that poet John Greenleaf Whittier died.

WITH NO POSSIBILITY of entering Boston's financial world and no social protection against unemployment or on-the-job injury, many immigrants turned to politics. Joining the political process increased the possibility of

Louis Dembitz Brandeis

OCCUPATION: Justice, U.S. Supreme Court

LIFETIME: 1856–1941

FAMILY: Son of Jewish immigrants from Bohemia, born in Louisville, Kentucky. Married Alice Goldmark, 1891. Two daughters.

ACCOMPLISHMENTS: Boston's "people's lawyer," representing ordinary citizens against corporations. Associate justice, U.S. Supreme Court, 1916–1939.

GREATEST CONTROVERSY: First Jew appointed to Supreme Court, which resulted in highly contentious confirmation hearings in Senate.

Justice and Mrs. Brandeis on his eighty-second birthday

"Experience should teach us to be most on our guard to protect liberty when the government's purposes are beneficent. Men born to freedom are naturally alert to repel invasion of their liberty by evil-doers. The greatest dangers to liberty lurk in insidious encroachment by men of zeal, well-meaning but without understanding."

a job with the city or a connection to social services, and thus offered the best avenue for improvement.

From his base at the Hendricks Club in the West End, near today's Fleet Center (formerly Boston Garden), Martin Lomasney became one of the most powerful men in Boston. Lomasney hated to be called a political boss; he was pleased when a journalist nicknamed him "the Mahatma" instead. A quiet man most comfortable working behind the scenes, for most of his political life he was more powerful than any mayor, serving on Boston's

Roxbury-born John L. Sullivan (right) fighting Paddy Ryan, 1882. Commenting on the number of Irish in Boston, Sullivan said, "Boston's the greatest Sullivan town in the whole world. . . . If you was to take the name of Sullivan out of the Boston Telephone Directory, it 'ud look like the Bible would if it didn't say nothing about God."

Board of Aldermen and Common Council and in the state legislature, state senate, and 1920 state constitutional convention. He promoted the building of North Station and Boston Garden and lowered the price of natural gas for city residents. When a disgruntled city contractor tried to assassinate Lomasney in City Hall, the Mahatma quipped, "The people didn't think an awful lot of Aldermen, but they didn't think we ought to be shot without a fair trial."

Lomasney insisted that the city publish a directory of all its employees so he could keep track of what jobs were available. He required of a constituent seeking a job only that the man vote and that he be competent. "Now he sent a Negro, again a Hebrew or an Italian, to the city government," the *New York Sun* noted, "and thus has held the allegiance of those who regarded themselves almost as a submerged people." When muckraking journalist Lincoln Steffens researched urban corruption in Boston, he heard that Lomasney was the worst of the bosses. But after seeing how effectively and how honestly Lomasney conducted his affairs, Steffens concluded that the Mahatma of the West End was actually one of Boston's best.

Across the harbor in East Boston, thousands of immigrants had debarked from the Cunard Steamship Line and climbed the golden stairs from the dock onto Webster Street. As in the West End, politics and hard work became the way to a new life. Two Irish immigrants, Patrick and Brigid Kennedy, met at sea and married shortly after arriving. Both died shortly after reaching their promised land, but not before they had a son, Patrick Joseph Kennedy, who grew up to own a tavern in East Boston. From this base Patrick became a political leader, a contemporary of Lomasney. Kennedy's son, Joseph P. Kennedy, graduated from Boston Latin and Harvard College, and in 1914 married the daughter of another neighborhood political boss, former Boston mayor John Fitzgerald, known as

MARTIN LOMASNEY

PATRICK J. KENNEDY
NODDLE ISLAND LEADER

JOHN F. FITZGERALD
KNOWS WHAT HE WANTS.

Three caricatures by *Boston Post* cartoonist William Norman Ritchie (1866–1947), who for half a century lampooned political figures and who, because he was ambidextrous, was able to draw two cartoons simultaneously.

1. The West End Mahatma, Martin Lomasney

2. East Boston's Patrick J. Kennedy

3. The North End's John Fitzgerald, congressman and Boston mayor

"Honey Fitz." Fitzgerald's parents, like Kennedy's, came from Ireland during the migration of the 1840s. Like Kennedy in East Boston, Fitzgerald began his political career in the North End by opening a tavern. He was elected to Congress in 1894, the year after his daughter Rose was baptized in St. Stephen's Church. Political power was passing from the hands of the Brahmins to the hands of immigrants. Would the new Bostonians preserve the legacy of the Yankees?

The answer came in 1895 when Congressman Fitzgerald, who as a boy had once sold newspapers on the corner of Beacon and Park Streets, became interested in having the USS *Constitution* return to Boston for the centennial of her launch. He went to see the ship at its berth in Portsmouth, New Hampshire. Horrified to see that the navy had removed the masts and built a barracks on the top deck and to learn that the hull leaked so badly it was impossible to move the ship, Fitzgerald went to work immediately. Using his political power to get money from Congress to restore *Constitution*, he also enlisted the support of Charles Francis Adams, president of the Massachusetts Historical Society. These two men—the grandson of John Quincy Adams (and great-grandson of John Adams) and the grandfather of John Fitzgerald Kennedy—worked together

An immigrant boy salutes his country on a ship approaching Boston in the 1890s. This photograph offers a more positive image of immigration than the drawing from the 1850s found on page 54.

to save USS *Constitution* and bring it back to Boston.

Immigrants brought much with them but also embraced what they found in the New World. As a schoolgirl in Chelsea, Russian Jewish immigrant Mary Antin did not feel her American-born classmates appreciated George Washington as they should—or as she did. To make them appreciate what Washington meant to a Jewish child from Russia, she wrote a poem in tribute to him. Published in one of Boston's papers, it launched Antin on a literary quest, which she followed with *The Promised Land,* a memoir of her journey from Russia to the New World, with its electric lights and free education.

Her own palace, her favorite refuge, was the Boston Public Library, opened in 1895 with the words *Free to All* inscribed above the door. In the Boston Public Library, Antin gloried in the treasures of Bates Hall, the reading room, named for a former Bostonian, Joshua Bates. Like Benjamin Franklin, Bates had left an impoverished Boston childhood to seek opportunities elsewhere. He became a successful London banker, working for Baring Brothers. The city of Boston applied to Baring Brothers when it was trying to finance its massive sewage treatment project. Among the documents sent was the modest proposal to build a public library. Bates, recalling his own struggle for an education when a boy in Boston, became interested and eventually became the Boston Public Library's first benefactor. He and Mary Antin would be pleased to see how well his bequest

Mary Antin

PROFESSION: Writer

LIFETIME: 1881–1949

FAMILY: Born in Russia. Emigrated to Boston with mother and three siblings to join her father, 1894. Married paleontologist Amadeus William Grabau, 1901. One daughter.

ACCOMPLISHMENTS: First book, translation of Yiddish letter written to her uncle that gives account of voyage to America, published as *From Plotzk to Boston* (1899). *The Promised Land* (1912) and *They Who Knock at Our Gates* (1914) each sold more than 100,000 copies.

GREATEST CHALLENGE: Separated from her husband, suffered nervous breakdown and never wrote again.

Mary Antin

"America is the youngest of the nations, and inherits all that went before it in history. And I am the youngest of America's children, and into my hands is given all her price-less heritage, to the last white star espied through the telescope, to the last great thought of the philosopher. Mine is the whole majestic past, and mine is the shining future."

continues to benefit immigrants and natives, students and professors, lawyers and homeless people, who continue to use Bates Hall.

∽ ∽ ∽

IN ADDITION TO the intellectual refuge created in the Boston Public Library, the city created an environmental refuge in this period. Frederick Law Olmsted, the country's foremost landscape architect and designer of New York City's Central Park, came to Boston in 1878 charged with creating an

Frederick Law Olmsted (1822–1903), creator of the Emerald Necklace, a comprehensive system of urban parks for Boston. Olmsted also designed New York's Central Park.

entire urban park system. Olmsted's Emerald Necklace runs from the Common, the oldest urban park in the nation, through the Public Garden, along Commonwealth Avenue, through the Fenway to Jamaica Plain, and finally connects with Franklin Park in Roxbury. Olmsted designed his parks to be oases in crowded urban neighborhoods—from the Emerald Necklace, which he planned to connect by way of Columbia Road with South Boston's Marine Park, to East Boston's beautiful Wood Island Park across the harbor.

After Olmsted's death in 1903, a state commission expanded his vision, creating a swath of public parklands surrounding the city, from the Blue Hills in the south to Revere Beach in the north. These open landscapes within and around the city would bring together Boston's diverse populations. The entire idea was so bold and farsighted, the commissioners displayed a one-ton plaster model of the Metropolitan Park System at the 1900 Paris Exposition.

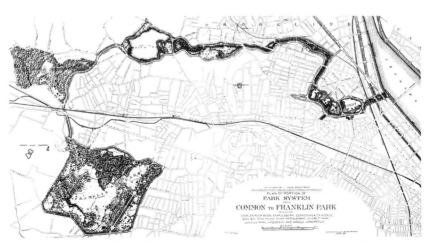

Olmsted's plan for the Emerald Necklace, stretching from Boston Common to Franklin Park, January 1894

Mary Baker Eddy

PROFESSION: Spiritual leader

LIFETIME: 1821–1910

FAMILY: Born in Bow, New Hampshire. Married George Washington Glover, 1843 (died 1844). Widowed while pregnant with her only child. Married Daniel Patterson, 1853, who would not let her son live with them. Patterson ran off with another woman, 1866, and they divorced, 1873. Married Asa Gilbert Eddy, 1877 (died 1882).

ACCOMPLISHMENTS: Founder of Christian Science Church after miraculous recovery from near-fatal fall on ice in 1866 propelled her to investigate spiritual powers of healing. Published *Science and Health* (1875). Founded *Christian Science Monitor* (1908).

Mary Baker Eddy

"The time for thinkers has come;
and the time for revolutions,
ecclesiastic and social, must come."

BOSTON WAS A CITY with many communities bounded by geography and ethnicity. History and the physical landscape held together these diverse neighborhoods. The ideas of Bostonians, rooted in history, continued to shape the wider world. A miraculous recovery from a slip on the ice in 1866 propelled Mary Baker Eddy to consider the role of spiritual strength in healing. In 1875 she published *Science and Health* and founded the Christian Science Church.

One of the most notable Bostonians of the era, William Monroe Trotter, published *The Guardian* in the same printing office where Garrison had once printed *The Liberator*. Trotter's father had served in the all-black Massachusetts Fifty-fifth Regiment, and young Trotter, born after the war, had graduated from Harvard in 1895.

William Monroe Trotter

OCCUPATION: Journalist

LIFETIME: 1872–1934

FAMILY: Born in Ohio, reared in Boston. Son of James Trotter, veteran of Massachusetts Fifty-fifth Regiment. Married Geraldine Louise Prindell,1899 (died in flu epidemic, 1918).

ACCOMPLISHMENTS: One of first African American students to graduate from Harvard, 1895. Founder of *The Guardian*, weekly paper for Boston's black community. Forced changes in film *Birth of a Nation* before it could be shown in Boston, 1915, and eventually prevented it from being shown at all, 1921.

GREATEST CONTROVERSIES: Arrested for challenging Booker T. Washington at Columbus Avenue Church, 1903. Criticized President Wilson at White House for segregating federal bureaucracy, 1914.

William Monroe Trotter

From his challenge to Booker T. Washington in 1903: *"Do you not know that the ballot is the only self-protection for any class of people in the country?"*

Trotter became a national spokesman for African Americans opposed to the accommodationist policies of Booker T. Washington, president of Tuskegee Institute in Alabama. When Washington spoke at the Columbus Avenue African Methodist Episcopal Zion Church in 1903, Trotter came to heckle. He charged Washington with accepting the racial violence of the South and with accepting segregation in return for his own share of patronage from the Alabama legislature. Should black people accept second-class status and give up their political and social rights? The Boston police arrested Trotter for starting a riot.

In the Charles Street Jail, Trotter had time to read *The Souls of Black Folk,* by another black intellectual from Massachusetts, W. E. B. DuBois, who had an even more devastating critique of the Washington program. After his release, Trotter met with DuBois, and the two began organizing the National Association for the Advancement of Colored People (NAACP), which sought full integration of African Americans into American society.

Trotter, Mary Antin, the Fitzgeralds, and the Kennedys all sought full inclusion into Boston society. Late in life, Joseph P. Kennedy remarked bitterly that though he had served as American ambassador to the Court of St. James, had one son die fighting for the United States in Europe, and had another representing Massachusetts in the U.S. Senate, to many in the Boston business community he was still "an Irishman." This exclusive world proved most difficult to enter.

Edward Filene, the son of Jewish immigrants, became one of Boston's most successful and imaginative businessmen. Though he was a founder of the U.S. Chamber of Commerce, Filene later found himself excluded from business gatherings because he supported the New Deal.

IN THE SPRING OF 1920, thousands of immigrants and other working people in Boston believed they had found a path into the world of Boston's business elite. Every morning hundreds of people lined up on School Street to invest their savings with the Securities Exchange Company and its charming and charismatic founder, Charles Ponzi. Ponzi promised to double investments in ninety days through a complicated international scheme involving postal coupons and exchange rates. Ponzi did double his early investors' money, but he did it by paying them from funds that new investors were putting in. Ponzi, an Italian immigrant, soon left the North End for a Lexington mansion. As he arrived on School Street each

Cartoonist "Norman" (William Norman Ritchie) lampooned Charles Ponzi in the *Boston Post.*

Edward A. Filene

OCCUPATION: Retailer

LIFETIME: 1860–1937

FAMILY: Son of Jewish immigrants, born in Salem, Massachusetts. Never married.

ACCOMPLISHMENTS: Took over family's clothing store and turned it into largest department store in world. Created Filene's Basement. Chaired Massachusetts State Recovery Board during Depression.

GREATEST CONTROVERSIES: Unlike other business leaders, supported Franklin Roosevelt's New Deal. Though a founder of U.S. Chamber of Commerce, was refused a chance to speak at 1934 meeting when he proposed that the chamber consider ways of reforming its structure to keep up with changing times.

Edward A. Filene

"Democracy . . . is not a formula. It is a growth. It cannot be granted by a constitution. It must be developed out of the actual conditions of life."

morning in his chauffeured Bentley, he was greeted as a hero by crowds eager to give him their money. When a reporter asked Ponzi about history's great Italians, he noted that Christopher Columbus had discovered America, and that Guigliemo Marconi had invented the radio. "And Ponzi discovered money!" shouted an enthusiastic investor.

Arthur Barron, editor of an investment newsletter (now *Barron's*), criticized Ponzi's method. No investment could double in ninety days, he said. Barron also charged that an Italian immigrant like Ponzi could not understand the intricacies of capitalism. Ponzi responded that Italians had invented banking, and the ethnic slur brought in more investors—Italians,

Jews, Irish, African Americans. Two Boston police officers came to Ponzi's office to check his credentials. They left as investors.

Ponzi's scheme collapsed as suddenly as it had appeared. His press agent—Ponzi was one of the first to hire a publicist—began to wonder why, if Ponzi's investments returned 100 percent interest, he kept his money in banks, which paid only 5 percent? The *Boston Post* looked into Ponzi's past and learned that the years Ponzi had spent in Montreal, where he claimed to have been studying international finance, he had actually been in prison for check fraud. Ponzi went to jail again and was eventually deported to Italy; the *Boston Post* won a Pulitzer Prize for its investigation; six banks that had lent money to Ponzi on the promise of his continued wealth collapsed; and thousands of investors—immigrants mostly, many of whom had mortgaged their homes or turned their life savings over to Ponzi—were ruined.

PONZI OFFERED ENTRY into the world of finance. James Michael Curley stormed the Boston political world. Born in the Irish slums of Roxbury, Curley formed a political organization that took on all—the Brahmin bankers of State Street and the other urban ward bosses like Lomasney, whom he dismissed as "chowderheads." For half a century Curley dominated Boston politics, elected to the Board of Aldermen in 1903 when he was in jail and winning his last term as mayor in 1945 when he was under federal indictment. But Curley was not a petty criminal. For many Bostonians this self-described "mayor of the poor," who had gone to jail for helping a friend, was a hero. They chose him four times to be mayor, twice sent him to Congress, and once elected him governor of Massachusetts.

As mayor, Curley centralized patronage in his office, making the ward bosses less important. Curley's administrations delivered services to the neighborhoods, building parks, bath houses, and schools; improving roads; and

Two of twentieth-century Boston's most influential leaders, James Michael Curley and Richard Cardinal Cushing, exchange pleasantries on Broadway in South Boston. Curley was in the midst of his last successful campaign for mayor; Cushing, a native of South Boston, had just become archbishop.

Fannie Farmer

OCCUPATION: Cooking teacher, cookbook author

LIFETIME: 1857–1915

FAMILY: Born in Boston. Never married.

ACCOMPLISHMENTS: Became director of alma mater, Mary J. Lincoln's Boston Cooking School, 1894. Published *Boston Cooking School Cookbook* (1896). Founded own cooking school, 1902.

GREATEST CHALLENGES: Paralytic stroke in high school forced her to discontinue education and enroll in cooking school. As director of Boston Cooking School and her own Miss Farmer's School of Cookery, trained housewives rather than professional chefs.

Fannie Farmer

"I certainly feel that the time is not far distant when a knowledge of the principles of diet will be an essential part of one's education. Then mankind will eat to live, will be able to do better mental and physical work, and disease will be less frequent."

building a tunnel under Boston Harbor. But Curley joyfully alienated business leaders, and his administrations could not solve the problems of the Depression or of Boston's long economic decline.

Defeated for reelection by city clerk John B. Hynes in 1949, Curley retired to his mansion overlooking Jamaica Pond. He tweaked his Yankee neighbors by having shamrocks cut into the shutters, while they asked how he could afford such a mansion on the mayor's salary. Curley ran three more times, unsuccessfully, for mayor. More than two decades after his death, the city finally decided to honor its most famous mayor with a statue. But

Curley's legacy was so complicated—was he the bold Robin Hood challenging the status quo or the corrupt demagogue who bankrupted the city?—that he needed two statues. Both Curleys now hold court across from Faneuil Hall. One is the bold "Young Jim" striding forward to take on the Brahmin elite; the other, an older man, sits on a park bench reflecting on his life and legacy. Novelist Edwin O'Connor immortalized Curley and his political world in the novel *The Last Hurrah*, which so touched the retired mayor that Curley wrote his own memoir, which he called *I'd Do It Again*.

BOSTON'S POLITICAL AND FINANCIAL WORLDS remained divided by ethnicity and social class. But in other areas, Bostonians in the 1920s and 1930s began to come together. In 1929 Arthur Fiedler, the son of a Boston Symphony violinist, conducted the first Boston Pops concert outdoors on the Charles River Esplanade. Fiedler introduced these outdoor concerts, notably on July 4, and for the next fifty years as conductor of the "Pops," Fiedler brought music out of the concert hall to wherever people gathered to listen. Another Bostonian, Leonard Bernstein, graduated from Roxbury's Garrison Elementary School and Boston Latin,

ABOVE: Mayor Curley and congressional candidate John F. Kennedy flank Governor Maurice Tobin at the 1946 V.F.W. Convention. Tobin, who had defeated Curley for mayor in 1937 and 1939, served as U.S. Secretary of Labor in the Truman administration.

BELOW: Leonard Bernstein, product of the Boston public school system, taking a bow

defying his family's wishes that he go into business. Instead Bernstein chose music, despite an uncle's warning that it was not a suitable career for a Jewish

Edwin O'Connor

Edwin O'Connor

OCCUPATION: Novelist

LIFETIME: 1918–1968

FAMILY: Born in Providence, Rhode Island. Married Vieniette Caswell Wiel, 1962. One stepson.

ACCOMPLISHMENTS: Based second novel, *The Last Hurrah* (1956), on life of Boston politician and mayor James Michael Curley. Won Pulitzer Prize for *The Edge of Sadness* (1961).

CHALLENGES: Threatened with libel suit by Mayor Curley, who later decided he liked the character based on him, Frank Skeffington, in *The Last Hurrah*.

Nathaniel Gardiner watching Skeffington's funeral in *The Last Hurrah*: "*Skeffington had gone, and it was as if a part of the city itself had gone: a part of the city which Gardiner had both liked and deplored. . . . And now it was gone, and Gardiner, too, was an old man who would soon be going; the question he asked himself now was: Who and what is to follow us? And because he loved this city, he would not have mourned the passing of the old if he could have seen even the promise of improvement in the new. But he could not. . . . The old buccaneer, for all his faults, had at least been a capable, vivid, unforgettable personality; he had been succeeded by the spearhead of a generation of ciphers.*"

boy. Bernstein's long affiliation with the Boston Symphony at its summer home in Tanglewood began in 1940, where he became assistant to conductor Serge Koussevitsky. Composer and long-time conductor of the New York Philharmonic, Bernstein and his music transcended narrow boundaries. Fittingly, he dedicated his Third Symphony, *Kaddish* (1963), to the memory of a child of Irish Catholic Boston, John F. Kennedy. In 1971 Bernstein composed and conducted his *Mass* for the opening of the Kennedy Center in Washington.

In sports, as in music, Bostonians began to transcend the boundaries of race, class, and ethnicity through such amateur sporting events as the Boston Marathon. By the 1930s, the marathon, begun by New York runners in 1897, the year after South Boston's James Brendan Connolly won the first gold medal in the modern Olympics, had a new champion in Boston's Johnny Kelley. In the first decades of the century, Bostonians built new sporting palaces, notably Harvard Stadium in Brighton (the country's first steel-reinforced concrete building) in 1902 and what is now the oldest ice hockey rink in the world, the Boston Arena (now the Matthews Arena at Northeastern University), in 1909. The Boston Bruins (one of the National Hockey League's original teams) played at the Boston Arena from their birth in 1924 until 1928, when they moved into their new home at the Boston Garden—and promptly won the Stanley Cup.

Professional baseball came to Boston in 1876 with the creation of the Braves, who had the best record in baseball five times in the 1890s. When the rival American League was born in 1901, Boston had a new team, the Red Sox, who won the first World Series over the Pittsburgh Pirates in 1903. The Red Sox opened their new home at Fenway Park in 1912. The Red Sox went on to win five world championships with a pitching staff that included Cy Young and left-hander Babe Ruth, who played the outfield on days he did not pitch. Ruth set a baseball record with twenty-nine home runs in 1919, a record one Boston sportswriter predicted would never be broken. But that winter Ruth was sold to the struggling New York Yankees, and though his wife continued to live on their Sudbury farm, Ruth became a New York slugger.

Baseball and hockey captured the imaginations of Bostonians more easily than did football, though Boston had the first organized football club in the United States. The Oneidas, drawn from the elite high schools in the Civil War years, played what Americans now call soccer. American-style football arrived in 1929 with the Boston Bulldogs, which changed their name

1. Johnny Kelley wins the Boston Marathon, 1935.

2. Boston Bruins, Stanley Cup champions, 1941–1942

3. The greatest pitcher ever to wear a Boston uniform, Cy Young pitched for both the Braves and the Red Sox, winning 511 games during his career. Here, a representative from the *Boston Post* presents Young with an award on Cy Young Day, 1908.

4. Babe Ruth at Fenway Park, 1933. The Boston Red Sox have not won a World Series since this man was sold to the New York Yankees.

5. Ted Williams, the greatest hitter who ever lived, enlists in the U.S. navy, 1942.

6. Jackie Robinson. The Red Sox did give Robinson a tryout in 1946 but decided he would not be a major league player. The Red Sox was the last major league team to sign a black player. Here Robinson visits with the Braves' Sam Jethroe at Braves Field, circa 1950.

to the Braves in 1932 in homage to the baseball team. The following year the team became the Redskins in tribute to their Native American coach, Lone Star Dietz. Though alumni and students of Harvard (Rose Bowl winner, 1920) or Boston College (Sugar Bowl champion, 1941) followed their school teams, Bostonians did not take readily to professional football. The Redskins lost the championship to the New York Giants in 1936, after which the team left Boston for Washington, where it enjoyed more success.

Boston's baseball teams also struggled. The Red Sox owners chose not to rebuild Fenway Park's left-field grandstand when it burned in 1926. The Red Sox reached a nadir in 1932, losing 111 games and drawing only 180,000 fans during the season. Tom Yawkey of South Carolina bought the struggling team in 1933. When a fire nearly destroyed Fenway Park in January 1934, Yawkey had it rebuilt in time to open the season, and then began the longer process of rebuilding the team. Braves owner Emil Fuchs brought Babe Ruth back to

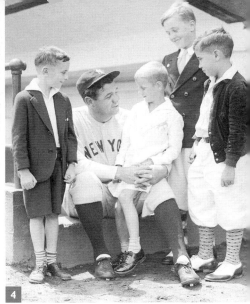

Boston in the twilight of the slugger's career, though Ruth retired in 1935 when he learned Fuchs did not plan to make him the team's manager. The all-star game hosted by the Boston Braves in 1936 has the distinction of having the lowest attendance ever, with 15,000 empty seats at Braves Field (now Nickerson Field at Boston University). When Ted Williams joined the Red Sox in 1939, the city gained a true champion, even though a championship still proved elusive. The following year, attendance at Fenway Park broke the record set in 1909.

WAS IT ONE BOSTON, knit together out of many diverse elements, as John Winthrop had hoped? Fitzgerald's work to save *Constitution*, Bernstein and Fiedler bringing people together with music, Bostonians joining together to cheer their teams suggest the possibility. Or was it many Bostons, a network of separate communities each preserving its own past: Yankee versus immigrant, black versus white, Christian versus Jew? Bostonians who lived during the late nineteenth and early twentieth centuries did make remarkable efforts to bring all together into one community.

the new boston

BOSTON'S IMPRESSIVE CULTURAL RESOURCES obscured the city's decline during most of the twentieth century. Boston did not escape the problems or changes of the rest of American society—the Great Depression, the spread to suburbs in the 1950s, the racial tensions of the 1960s and 1970s—but it had some intrinsic problems of its own. New York became the nation's commercial center in the nineteenth century, and the textile mills of Lowell and Lawrence had moved south to find cheaper labor. Pollution, overfishing, and foreign competition drove the fishing industry into collapse in the 1980s. The

The Leonard P. Zakim Bunker Hill Bridge, in a photo by Margot Balboni

city's traditional sources of new wealth disappeared, and in the 1950s, for the first time since the British forced people out in 1774, Boston's population declined.

The automobile and the GI Bill of Rights helped move people out of the city after World War II. Returning veterans were given low-interest housing, making it possible to buy or build a house rather than rent an apartment. Boston's suburbs expanded, though the city remained the place to work.

The GI Bill also changed the American workforce by guaranteeing veterans a college education. The United States was the world's leading industrial power before the war, and Boston's schools trained most children of blue-collar workers for blue-collar jobs. For example, young John Joseph "Joe" Moakley from South Boston went to South Boston High, where the specialty was sheet-metal work. Moakley earned his certificate there and would have spent the rest of his working days as a sheet-metal worker had it not been for the war. After returning from the South Pacific, he had an opportunity to go to college thanks to the GI Bill. He later entered politics and served for thirty years in Congress. Others became accountants, doctors, stockbrokers, college professors, and teachers. New England no longer had the industrial base that made Boston boom in the nineteenth century,

Carroll Sheehan of Dorchester, president of Suffolk University's graduating class of 1949, and Suffolk President Walter Burse thank Congressman John F. Kennedy for the GI Bill. Sheehan went on to become the state commerce commissioner.

but Boston in the late twentieth century maintained its position as a financial center, in large part because of the men and women supported in their educations by the GI Bill.

By opening college up to veterans, the GI Bill changed the nature of higher education. Boston and its surrounding communities today are home to more than fifty colleges and universities. Nearly a quarter of a million people from around the world attend college in greater Boston every year. But before World War II, college was reserved mainly for the elite. With a college education available to everyone who had served in the armed forces, some Boston schools that had been on the brink of closing suddenly flourished. By the turn of the twenty-first century, education would be crucial to Boston's economy.

Boston's colleges and financial institutions have transformed American society by bringing together ideas and capital. During World War II, researchers at Raytheon helped develop radar, and from that innovation came the microwave oven. At the Dana Farber Cancer Institute, doctors have worked to cure the scourge of cancer. In the late 1960s, acoustical engineers working with computer experts at Bolt, Beranek and Newman developed a system to allow computers to talk with each other, an innovation that resulted in the Internet.

BOSTON'S INNOVATORS AND CREATIVE MINDS have made wondrous breakthroughs, but the mid-twentieth century will also be remembered for its failures. Boston's political leaders, led by Mayor John B. Hynes and Boston College President W. Seavey Joyce, eager to put the Curley era behind them, embarked on a series of programs to transform the city and to create a "New Boston" that would energize the future rather than venerate the past. Government—city, state, and federal—and private institutions— banks, developers, and colleges—pushed forward a dizzying number of projects to change the city. The Central Artery was cut through downtown;

the "New York" streets of the South End, the neighborhood of the West End, and the Scollay Square area were demolished in order to renew the city; and Logan Airport was expanded until it dominated East Boston.

The Central Artery was built in the 1950s to relieve Boston's traffic congestion. City officials and experts believed that traffic would flow smoothly through the old city on the elevated highway. Instead, with its twenty-seven exit and entrance ramps in a two-mile span, the elevated highway made traffic worse and displaced ten thousand residents as it cut the city apart. The artery walled off the North End from downtown, cut off downtown from the waterfront, and tightly surrounded Chinatown with acres of asphalt and entrance ramps. The Chinese Merchants Association building, proudly built in the early 1950s as a permanent symbol of success in their new country, was capriciously sliced in half by the new highway. And with all this social dislocation, by the 1980s the highway carried three times as many cars as it was designed to. For hours every day, traffic sat idling on the expressway, poisoning the air and the tempers of thousands of drivers.

The planners of the New Boston in the 1950s, hoping to undo the damage of the Curley years, set about erasing much of Boston's past. They decided that the South End's "New York" streets—Albany, Oneida,

The Central Artery swallows up the city as it makes its way south, September 1954.

1. Mayor John B. Hynes begins the process of "urban renewal" by demolishing the "New York" Streets neighborhood in Boston's South End. Standing next to Hynes is Congressman John W. McCormack.

2. Eighteenth- and nineteenth-century buildings, their families evicted, await demolition in Boston's West End.

3. South End artist Allan Crite's *Burning and Digging* gives a different view of urban renewal.

Seneca, Oswego, Rochester—were a "blighted" neighborhood and that the land would be better used as an industrial area. The city demolished the housing and cleared the residents, mainly African American working people, out of the area. The city also deemed the working-class West End, a diverse neighborhood of 3,500 Jewish, Italian American, and African American families, as "blighted." The tenement homes were demolished and replaced with high-rise luxury housing. In like fashion, the city decided to demolish Scollay Square, home to vaudeville houses, boarding houses, taverns, and restaurants that had been popular haunts for sailors during the war. Scollay Square was replaced by Government Center, where Boston's new city hall and federal and state office buildings were built. One city councilor endorsed the project, saying he would "rather have visitors to Boston look at things they see in Miami or New York—bright shiny tax-producing buildings, rather than some ugly building where William Lloyd Garrison once published *The Liberator*."

This vision of a shiny New Boston that looked like Miami or New York did not stop with the downtown. East Boston, home to generations of Irish and Italian immigrants and their descendants, had lived with the airport since the 1920s. From a small airstrip on landfill off Jeffries Point, Logan International Airport (named for World War I General Edward Lawrence Logan of South Boston) had expanded after World War II, absorbing Governors Island, Bird Island, Apple Island, and all the tidal flats between.

Other cities, such as Washington and Chicago, had built larger airports outside the city when their original downtown airports could expand no more. But the growing political power of Boston's suburbs prevented this option, so jets from Logan continue to screech over the city's neighborhoods and its historic sites: Castle Island, Old North Church, Dorchester Heights. In the late 1960s, when the airport did need to expand, it took Wood Island Park, an urban oasis designed by Frederick Law Olmsted. When Logan threatened to take more of East Boston, the neighbors resisted. Mothers of East Boston's Maverick Street, led by the tough but savvy Anna DeFronzo, took to the streets, blocking bulldozers and construction vehicles and preventing the airport from taking another inch of the neighborhood. When the Metropolitan District Commission built a skating rink in East Boston in the 1980s, neighbors broke in, suspecting that the building was actually going to be an aircraft hanger for an eternally expanding Logan. Years of acrimony forced the Massachusetts Port Authority (Massport), which administers Logan, to build the beautiful new Piers Park on the waterfront, connected with the East Boston Greenway that was transformed out of the old railroad lines. But goodwill has been difficult to maintain.

AN ATMOSPHERE OF DISTRUST also underlay Boston's most explosive event since the 1770s, the busing crisis of the 1970s. The Boston public school system, the oldest in the nation, was crumbling by the 1950s. Many dedicated, gifted teachers continued to teach in the Boston public schools. But the school department bureaucracy, staffed through political patronage, responded more to the needs of itself and its patrons than to the needs of Boston's students. The department systematically allocated fewer resources

Louise Day Hicks

OCCUPATION: Lawyer

LIFETIME: 1916–2003

FAMILY: Born in South Boston. Daughter of Judge William Day (for whom South Boston's Day Boulevard is named). Married John Hicks, 1942. Two children.

ACCOMPLISHMENTS: Graduated from Boston University Law School at age thirty-six. Elected to Boston School Committee, 1962–1967. First woman finalist in Boston mayor's race, 1967 (lost to Kevin White). Elected to city council, 1969; elected to Congress to succeed John McCormack, 1970. First woman president of Boston City Council, 1976.

GREATEST CONTROVERSY: Opposed forced busing to achieve racial balance in schools

Louise Day Hicks

"You know where I stand."

to schools in the minority communities of Roxbury and Dorchester than to those in communities such as Hyde Park and West Roxbury. South End parents tried a school boycott in 1963 to protest the system's inequity, and in 1965 the state Racial Imbalance Law mandated that schools in cities with significant minority populations needed to have racial balance. This controversial law seemed to mandate school desegregation. City councilor and school committee member Louise Day Hicks of South Boston was nearly elected mayor in 1967 on a platform opposed to mandatory desegregation. "You know where I stand" was Mrs. Hicks's slogan, though she narrowly lost to Massachusetts Secretary of State Kevin H. White, who took office as Boston began a decade of violence.

The city and the school department failed to heed the demands for an improved education for minority students. At the same time, growing tensions between black and white Americans were finding expression in local and national outbreaks of violence. In response to a series of riots in the Grove Hall area of Roxbury in 1967 and the assassination of Dr. Martin Luther King Jr. in 1968, a group of Boston bankers decided to do what they could to improve living conditions for African Americans. The bankers created the Boston Bank Urban Renewal Group, or BBURG, to lend money to African Americans seeking to buy homes. BBURG drew a "red line" around Blue Hill Avenue and Gallivan Boulevard in Mattapan and Dorchester. In this district, low-interest loans were made to qualified African Americans. In 1960, the neighborhood was home to 70,000 Jewish residents; by 1971, only 1,500 Jews remained.

Mayor John Collins (right) and Boston Redevelopment Authority chair Edward Logue discuss the demolition of Scollay Square, making way for the new Government Center.

The Boston School Committee, rather than responding to pressure from parents, students, or the law by providing more resources or building magnet schools, instead dug in its heels. When the department had an opportunity to build a new school, it passed over ethnically diverse Dorchester, Mattapan, and the South End to build a school in nearly all-white Allston. The new Allston school convinced frustrated African American parents that their children would never be given a quality education in the Boston school system. They sued the school committee. Federal Judge W. Arthur Garrity Jr. ruled in 1974 that the Boston Public Schools had maintained a segregated system. He appointed a "master" from Cambridge to draw up a plan to base a child's school assignment on his or her race. To balance the schools racially, children would be bused between Roxbury

Swimming at East Boston's Wood Island Park. Once one of Frederick Law Olmsted's urban oases, it was obliterated by Logan Airport.

Mel King

OCCUPATION: Community
activist, college professor

LIFETIME: b. 1927

FAMILY: Born in South End,
one of eight children of
immigrants from Barbados and
Guyana. Married to Joyce King.
Six children.

ACCOMPLISHMENTS: Organized
protests that led to creation of Tent
City, affordable housing in Boston's
South End. Helped develop the
Urban School and Boston's Thomp-
son Academy, on Thompson Island.
Representative to Massachusetts
legislature, 1973–1983. Candidate
for mayor of Boston, 1983. Founder
of Community Fellows program at
MIT. Founded Rainbow Coalition,
which has merged with Green
Party to become Massachusetts
Rainbow Party.

GREATEST CHALLENGES:
Became community activist
seeking to change society without
violence. Arrested in protest at site
of Tent City, 1968.

Mel King, by Channing Thieme

"Love is the question and the answer."

and South Boston, Jamaica Plain and Charlestown, and Dorchester and
West Roxbury.

Violent protests in Charlestown and South Boston followed the court
order. The community activists found themselves pitted against one another rather than against the common threats to all Boston neighborhoods.
Mel King of the South End, whose family had been displaced when the

"New York" streets were razed, Raymond Flynn of South Boston, and airport opponent Elvira "Pixie" Palladino of East Boston became leaders of different factions. Flynn and King ran against each other for mayor in 1983.

Ray Flynn, the first mayor from South Boston, recognized the need to heal the city's racial divide. The black residents of Roxbury, Dorchester, and the South End considered seceding from Boston and forming the independent city of Mandela. Flynn began to work closely with neighborhood leaders in all Boston's communities. Though it cost him political support in his own neighborhood, Flynn pushed ahead with the integration of public housing units in the city and allocated more resources to parks in the neighborhoods. But control of the public schools was out of his hands. The system was more geared to racial balance than to education. By the 1990s more than 90 percent of the Boston public school students in all neighborhoods were minority students, but they still were bused all around the city to ensure illusory racial balance. With no power in choosing where their children went to school, middle-class parents of all races continued to leave the city.

By the early 1990s, it was apparent that public education in Massachusetts was in crisis. State lawmakers—led by Senate President William Bulger of South Boston, a persistent advocate of charter schools and state aid to parochial schools—responded with the Education Reform Act, which mandated testing of schoolchildren to determine how much they were learning and how well the schools were teaching them. The test results showed that although some of the public schools were doing quite well, many were doing very poorly. The Education Reform Act also promised more state aid to schools and allowed communities of parents to create so-called charter schools, alternatives to the public schools that would be under the control of parents and teachers rather than school administrators.

The First Lady of Roxbury, Melnea Cass (1896–1978). An active supporter of many forms of civil rights—for women, senior citizens, and people displaced by urban renewal—Cass (center) is shown here receiving an award honoring her efforts.

William M. Bulger

OCCUPATION: Public servant, lawyer, university president

LIFETIME: b. 1934

FAMILY: Born in Dorchester, one of six children. Married Mary Foley, 1960. Nine children.

William Bulger

ACCOMPLISHMENTS: Served in Massachusetts House of Representatives, 1961–1970. As freshman state representative, sponsored nation's first law to protect abused children. Served in Massachusetts Senate, 1971–1995, from 1978 to 1995 as president (longer than any other person in state history). President, University of Massachusetts, 1995–2003.

GREATEST CONTROVERSY: Older brother is James "Whitey" Bulger (1929–??), a powerful criminal and ultimately an FBI informant. Political opponents have tried throughout William Bulger's career to tie him to his brother's criminal activities.

"But if politics demands hard work and inflicts pain, it also offers an occasional touch of poetry. It is at various times, and in varying degrees, the fount of realized hopes and the grief business, a sanguinary sport and the conjurer's art. . . . Politicians didn't invent any of that; democracy did."

FIASCOS—BUILDING THE CENTRAL ARTERY; destroying the West End, the "New York" streets, and Wood Island Park; the racial catastrophe of the 1960s and 1970s—all had consequences their sponsors could not have imagined. Most results were disastrous, but these episodes did provoke citizens to greater civic involvement. Just as the British attempt to raise revenue in the 1760s made Bostonians stand up and resist, and the failure to generate power with the Charles River forced the creation of the Back Bay, these fiascos also might ultimately produce better results.

From his office in the new city hall, Mayor White looked out on Faneuil Hall and Quincy Market, which by the late 1960s and early 1970s were seedy marketplaces. Scollay Square was gone, and now only these buildings remained. What should be done with these old markets? The visionaries of the New Boston wanted to destroy the old to build anew, but White had a different idea. He called in architects known for creating suburban shopping malls and proposed turning this area into an urban shopping center, keeping the historic character of the buildings. The new Faneuil Hall Marketplace, dedicated in 1976 as the nation celebrated its bicentennial, was a first step in revitalizing Boston's downtown. Other cities have copied Boston's idea, bringing new life to historic downtown or waterfront buildings.

After the Central Artery had cut its swath through the North End, downtown, and Chinatown, highway planners prepared to bring to life their second project, a "Southwest Corridor" to carry Interstate 95 through the Back Bay, Roxbury, Jamaica Plain, and Hyde Park. Residents of those neighborhoods, seeing the devastation caused by the Central Artery, engaged in some of the most creative acts of civil disobedience since the Stamp Act. Ultimately Governor Francis Sargent declared a moratorium on highway building in the city. To improve public transportation, the state instead used the federal transportation money that Congress had appropriated for highways. State Transportation Secretary Fred Salvucci, a Brighton native who had advised Mayor Kevin White in opposing Logan Airport's expansion, had the idea to create a walking and biking trail along the Southwest Corridor, connecting the South End and Roxbury along another greenway.

ON THE CENTRAL ARTERY, the traffic nightmare continued to grow. Salvucci proposed a new underground highway that would lower the artery, thus reconnecting the North End and downtown with the waterfront. The so-called Big Dig project, behind schedule and over budget, has the potential to change Boston in a way no project has since the filling of the Back Bay in the nineteenth century. That project would not have happened if the original plan, to use the Charles River's tidal basin to generate power, had worked. The elegant Back Bay stands on the trash heap of a failed idea. And while the Central Artery, and the various other projects of the 1950s and 1960s, were imposed from above by community leaders who "knew best,"

Frederick P. Salvucci

OCCUPATION: Civil engineer

LIFETIME: Born in Brighton, 1940.

FAMILY: Married to Maryann Salvucci; three children.

ACCOMPLISHMENTS: Advisor to Boston Mayor Kevin White, 1975–1978. As Massachusetts Secretary of Transportation (1983–1990), planned Boston's Central Artery/Tunnel ("Big Dig") project.

GREATEST CHALLENGE: Primary planner of Big Dig project.

Fred Salvucci

"This is a city that's been created by man, by humans. When the English first got here, most of it was underwater. . . . Boston's a city that people have built. . . . And I find it exciting to see that continuing to happen."

the Big Dig from its inception has had to respond to its many critics. The project has been a collaborative process between and among the many different communities of Boston. So the Big Dig project, from the elegant Leonard P. Zakim Bunker Hill Bridge to the parkland that connects Faneuil Hall and the North End and gives breathing room to Chinatown, promises to build a better Boston for the future.

As the city was pushing forward in the 1960s with its plans for a New Boston, as the John Hancock and Prudential towers rose over the former railroad yards and the Massachusetts Turnpike, residents of the adjoining neighborhoods—particularly the South End—believed their housing needs were being ignored. In a vacant lot down the street from the proposed shopping mall at Copley Place, families in need of housing pitched tents to protest the city's failure to care for its residents. They camped at "Tent City" in 1968, maintaining a protest that kept the city from selling this parcel to developers. Finally, in 1991 a permanent Tent City opened. This new housing project rejected the failed public housing ideas of the past, which had simply called for warehousing the poor in high-rises. Instead, Tent City has created a community of its tenants that fits in so well with the surrounding streets that one can imagine it has always been there.

Diagonally across from Tent City, just across the Southwest Corridor Park in the Back Bay train station, is a statue of a Bostonian who would have taken great pride in the community action that led to these victories. A. Philip Randolph, editor, labor organizer, and African American intellectual, demanded in 1940 that the Roosevelt administration forbid defense contractors from discriminating on the basis of race. When the administration balked, Randolph proposed that 100,000 African Americans march on Washington, D.C., to demand equal employment opportunities. Fearing potential embarrassment, the administration yielded, creating the Fair Employment Practices Commission. Randolph did not march on Washington, but in 1963, when the Civil Rights Bill was stalled in Congress, Randolph suggested the idea to Martin Luther King

Jr., who had lived on Tremont Street during his own student days at Boston University, had met his wife, Coretta Scott, when she was a student at the New England Conservatory, and had preached at Roxbury's Twelfth Baptist Church. Randolph's idea led to the March on Washington in August 1963.

Martin Luther King Jr. on Boston Common. Just over a decade after completing his doctorate at Boston University, King returned to Boston to lead a civil rights march.

The irony is that while the bankers and political dreamers sought a New Boston by obliterating the old, in the city's neighborhoods men and women were building their own New Boston on the foundation set down by John Winthrop, Samuel Adams, and Martin Lomasney.

7

return to long wharf

FROM THE END OF LONG WHARF, we can see how the city continues to be transformed. The planes landing across the harbor continue to bring new Bostonians, still coming from Ireland and England and Italy, but also from Central America, Africa, and Asia, to transform and enrich the city.

Just east and south of the airport on Deer Island stand the egg-shaped sewage digesters. When the Massachusett lived here, Deer Island was named for the deer that swam to this outermost island of the inner harbor islands. In 1676 Deer Island was the final

Boston from Piers Park, East Boston

Massachusetts home for hundreds of Indians, taken prisoner during King Philip's War and sold as slaves in the West Indies. Almost two centuries later, in the 1850s, Suffolk County's prison and a quarantine hospital were built on the island. Many immigrants took sick on the rough Atlantic passage and died in the Deer Island hospital, their lives in the New World cut short. They lie buried on Deer Island. The egg-shaped sewage digesters now dominate the skyline; they also make Boston Harbor one of the cleanest urban harbors in the world.

Between Deer Island and Long Island, what was Kings Roads, the water entrance to the town in colonial Boston, is now President Roads; it is still the main shipping channel into the city. Long Island, at more than two hundred acres the harbor's largest, has housed hotels, a chronic disease hospital (more than two thousand victims of disease lie in unmarked graves), a homeless shelter, a Civil War training ground, and Cold War missile silos. Beyond Long Island is Georges Island, with its Civil War–era fort where Union soldiers trained and Confederate prisoners were held. Georges Island is now the centerpiece of the Boston Harbor Islands National Recreation Area.

Mayor Kevin H. White (center) with William M. Bulger, president of the state senate (right), and Congressman Joe Moakley. White gave this photo to Moakley with the inscription "Joe—Keep sending the money from Washington; Billy and I will spend it."

Dominating the harbor skyline is Spectacle Island, resurrected, like the harbor itself, from a century of being a garbage dump. The huge mounds of trash have been capped with excavations from the Big Dig, but not before archaeologists uncovered evidence of the island's past use as a Native American fishing ground. Today, the grassy slopes of Spectacle Island, laid out with walking trails, allow visitors to look out seaward and back toward the city in the kind of landscaped urban oasis Frederick Law Olmsted created a century ago. From Long Wharf, regular boat service to these islands allows the urban population to continue to enjoy the natural surroundings of the harbor.

The harbor's resurrection in the 1990s is the story of Boston's rediscovery of its treasures. The massive harbor cleanup and the preservation of the islands involved many committed individuals. Federal district judge A. David Mazzone ordered the Massachusetts Water Resources Authority (MWRA) in 1985 to begin the seemingly impossible task of cleaning the harbor, in accordance with the Clean Water Act of 1970. For the next fifteen years, Judge Mazzone oversaw the creation of Boston's new sewage treatment system, and Congressman John Joseph Moakley sought federal money to pay for the project.

As a boy growing up in the Old Harbor housing project and as a young lifeguard along the sandy strand of Carson Beach, Moakley remembered when the harbor was fit for swimming and when it was best found by following your nose. As a state senator in the 1960s, Moakley blocked plans to develop the harbor islands, instead having them made into a state park. After the 1988 election, when George H. W. Bush defeated Massachusetts Governor Michael Dukakis by pointing to Boston Harbor's filth, Moakley and U.S. Senator Edward M. Kennedy worked to secure federal money to clean the harbor. With a clean harbor, Moakley next moved to have the state park become a federal park, one of the few natural urban areas in the country.

From Long Wharf is seen the gleaming glass of the John Joseph Moakley Federal Courthouse on Fan Pier. The area stretching south of the Moakley

Courthouse is slated to become Boston's newest development, rising, much as the Back Bay did, on the edges of what had been an urban industrial wasteland. Moakley remembered dodging the freight trains on Fan Pier as a boy, trying to catch watermelons that fell from the cars. When the courthouse was named in his honor just a few months before his death, he thought of the "beautiful circle" his life had made, from a gritty urban youth to a respected and beloved statesman. The courthouse is one monument, and the harbor and its islands stand as another, fitting memorial to Joe Moakley and to all who have enjoyed them—Native American and immigrant—and all who will continue to enjoy them into the future.

From Long Wharf we can see far into the past, into the age of glaciers and geologic transformation, to the Massachusett people who fished in their Quonehassit, to Maverick and Blackstone and Winthrop, to the days of codfish and the rum trade, the Revolution and immigration, the China trade and clipper ships, industrial development and environmental destruction. Long Wharf remains, a vantage point from which to watch the continuing transformation of Boston.

Deer Island, 2001. After years of heavy pollution, Boston Harbor is now clean. The change in large part is due to the Deer Island sewage treatment facility in the foreground.

chronology

1600s

1617–1619	Plague devastates the Native American Massachusett population.
1624	Samuel Maverick establishes a fishing outpost on Noddle's Island, now East Boston.
1626[?]	Reverend William Blackstone settles on Beacon Hill.
1628	James Pemberton begins farming on George's Island.
1630	John Winthrop and fleet of Puritans land on Massachusetts shores.
1631	Boston is designated the capital of the Massachusetts Bay Colony.
1632	A smallpox epidemic devastates the Native American population. The first meetinghouse and burial ground are established at Roxbury.
1635	Boston Latin School, the first public school in North America, is founded.
1639	In Dorchester, the first school building in the country is built with grazing fees for Thompson's Island.
1645	Roxbury Latin School is founded.
1648–1650	James Blake builds a farmhouse in Dorchester, now the oldest surviving structure in Boston.
1660	Quaker Mary Dyer is executed for heresy on Boston Common.
1663	John Eliot, minister of First Church, Roxbury, publishes the first Bible in America, which is translated into the Algonkian language.
1688	Goodwife "Goody" Glover, accused of being a "slanderous old woman" and "obstinate in idolatry," is executed for witchcraft on Boston Common.
1689	Bostonians arrest Edmund Andros, sent by the king to govern Massachusetts.
1690	The population of Boston reaches 7,000.

1700s

1700	Minister Samuel Sewall writes *Selling of Joseph*, an antislavery tract. Boston population declines to 6,700.
1704	The *Boston News-Letter*, the first newspaper in America, is published.
1706	Benjamin Franklin is born on Milk Street.
1710	Boston population increases to 9,000.
1711–1715	Long Wharf is built, forming the longest pier in the New World.
1713	The Town House is built. Now called the Old State House, it is the second oldest public building in the United States.
1716	Boston Light is built on Little Brewster Island. It is the oldest lighthouse in North America and the only manned lighthouse in the United States.
1720	Boston population climbs to 12,000.
1721	A smallpox epidemic terrorizes Boston, infecting nearly 6,000 and killing 844. The African slave Onesimus suggests inoculation; Cotton Mather and others experiment with this controversial treatment.

Boston Light, Little Brewster Island, built in 1716

1730	Boston population reaches 13,000.
1737	The Charitable Irish Society is founded to relieve destitute Irish people.
1742	Faneuil Hall is given to the town by merchant Peter Faneuil.
1743	Boston population increases to 16,382.
1760	Boston population declines slightly to 15,631.
1765	August 14: The Sons of Liberty destroy Andrew Oliver's shop on Long Wharf, where they believe he is holding new British revenue stamps (issued through the Stamp Act).
	August 26: The Sons of Liberty ransack the home of Lieutenant Governor Thomas Hutchinson.
	Dr. James Baker of Dorchester starts a business grinding cocoa beans, creating the Baker Chocolate Company.
1767	England imposes the Townshend duties on certain imported trade goods.
1768	October 30: Two British regiments arrive in Boston; the siege of the Manufactory House occurs.
1769	August 14: More than three hundred Sons of Liberty meet in Dorchester.
1770	March 5: Boston Massacre takes place.
1773	Phillis Wheatley publishes her first book of poems, in London.

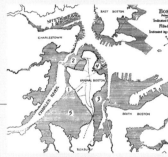

Filled areas of Boston and original shoreline, 1775

	December 16: Colonists dumped tea in Boston Harbor, in what became becomes known as the Boston Tea Party.
1774	In response to the Tea Party, Parliament closes the port of Boston and suspends the government of Massachusetts.
1775	April 19: British troops march to Lexington and Concord but are turned back.
	June 17: The British seize Breed's Hill after a day of fighting.
	July 3: George Washington arrives in Cambridge to take command of Continental forces.
	Boston population is approximately 16,000.
1776	March 17: British forces leave Boston.
	July 18: The Declaration of Independence is read publicly from the balcony of the Town House, now the Old State House.
	Boston population drops to 3,500.
1778	With the French fleet in the harbor, Bostonians do not observe "Pope's Day."
1784	The Massachusetts Bank is chartered.
1787	The Charles River Bridge, connecting Boston with Charlestown, opens.
1789	Abbé Claudius le Poterie begins regular celebrations of Roman Catholic Mass in a School Street chapel.
1790	President George Washington visits Boston.
	Boston population climbs to 18,320.
1797	The USS *Constitution* is launched at Hartt's Shipyard, North End.

1804   Judith Foster Saunders and Clementia Beach open Saunders' and Beach's Academy for Girls, Meeting House Hill, Dorchester.
Dorchester Neck, now South Boston, is annexed.

1806   The African Meeting House is built on Beacon Hill.
The Boston Athenaeum is founded.

1810   Boston population reaches 33,787.

1813   The *Boston Advertiser* begins publication. (The newpaper continues until a1929 merger with the *Daily Record*, which merges into the *Record American* in 1961 and then merges in 1972 to become the *Herald American*.)

1818   St Augustine's Chapel is built in South Boston. It is now the oldest Catholic church in Boston and one of the oldest remaining in New England.

1820   Boston population reaches 43,298.

1821   The Mill Dam is completed across Back Bay from Charles Street to Sewell's Point, Brookline, following what is now the line of Beacon Street from Boston Common to Kenmore Square.

1822   Boston becomes a city; Jonathan Phillips is elected its first mayor.

1824   The Marquis de Lafayette visits Boston.
The city acquires land that becomes the Public Garden.

1825   July 22: Police raid the Beehive, an Ann Street brothel.
Mayor Josiah Quincy designates South Boston for a public almshouse, prison, and insane asylum.

1826   The Boston Beer Company is founded in South Boston.

1827   Under the name Edgar A. Perry, eighteen-year-old Edgar Allan Poe enlists in the U.S. army at Castle Island.

1829   From his Brattle Street tailor shop, David Walker publishes *Appeal to the Colored Citizens of the World*.
The *Boston Pilot* begins publication.

1830   The *Boston Transcript* begins publication. (The newspaper continues until 1941.)

1831   The *Boston Post* begins publication. (The newspaper continues until 1956.)

1833   Sylvanus Thayer is sent to George's Island to plan fortifications. Over the next two decades, Fort Warren is built.

1834   An anti-Catholic mob burns the Ursuline Convent in Charlestown.

1837   The Broad Street riot breaks out between firefighters and marchers in an Irish funeral.

1839   Boston University is founded as a Methodist seminary in Vermont. Moves to Boston in 1867.

1841   Transcendentalists found Brook Farm, a cooperative utopian community, in West Roxbury.

1843   The Bunker Hill Monument is completed.
Ohabei Shalom, the first synagogue in Boston, opens on Charles Street. (The building now houses the Charles Street Playhouse.)

1844   The first Jewish cemetery is established, in East Boston.

African Meeting House, Beacon Hill, built in 1806

1845	The *Boston Traveler* begins publication. (It merges with the *Herald* in 1967.)
1847	The Custom House is completed.
1848	Forest Hills Cemetery, the second landscaped contemplative garden-style cemetery in the country, is established.
	On a campaign tour for Whig candidate Zachary Taylor, Illinois Congressman Abraham Lincoln speaks in Dorchester.
	The *Boston Herald* begins publication.
	The Boston Public Library is founded.
1850	Boston population equals 136,881.
1851	Donald McKay launches the *Flying Cloud*, the fastest clipper ship ever built, from his East Boston shipyard.
	The *Morning Journal* begins publication. (It merges with the *Herald* in 1917.)
1856	Boston's first public statue, of Benjamin Franklin, is dedicated on School Street.
1857	Harrison Loring builds iron steamships at his City Point, South Boston, shipyard.
1858–1882	The Back Bay is filled in.
1860	Boston population reaches 178,000.
1861	The "Tiger Battalion," Massachusetts Second Infantry stationed at Fort Warren, create a song, "John Brown's Body," which Julia Ward Howe of South Boston later revises into the "Battle Hymn of the Republic."
	The Massachusetts Institute of Technology is founded.
1862	The first football club in United States, the Oneida Club, begins playing on Boston Common.
1863	Boston College is founded on Harrison Avenue in the South End.
1865	New City Hall opens on School Street.
1866–1872	Fort Hill is leveled.
1867–1875	The new Cathedral of the Holy Cross is built in the South End.
1868	Roxbury is annexed to the City of Boston.
1870	Boston population increases to 251,000.
	The Massachusetts legislature charters the Museum of Fine Arts.
1872	A great fire destroys 800 buildings on sixty-five acres between Washington Street and the harbor.
	Julia Ward Howe establishes Mother's Day.
	Journalist John Boyle O'Reilly and Archbishop John Williams purchase *The Pilot*.
	The *Boston Globe* begins publication.
1873	St. Leonard's Church, the city's first Italian congregation, is founded in the North End.
1874	James Michael Curley is born in Roxbury.
	West Roxbury, Brighton, and Charlestown are annexed to the city.
1875	Louis Prang of Roxbury, the developer of chromolithography, prints the first Christmas cards in the United States.
	The Chinese Consolidated Benevolent Society is founded as the Chinese community begins to cluster in Oliver Place, now Ping On Alley.
	The Cathedral of the Holy Cross, South End, is dedicated.
	Boston population equals 341,919.

South Boston flats, now home to the John Joseph Moakley Courthouse, World Trade Center, and new Boston Convention Center

1876	In a laboratory near Scollay Square, Alexander Graham Bell sends the first message over a telephone: "Mr. Watson, come here, I want you."
	The Museum of Fine Arts opens in Copley Square.
	Leopold Morse is the first Jew elected to Congress from the Boston area.
1878	Frederick Law Olmsted begins creating a comprehensive park plan for Boston.
	Emerson College is founded.
1882	South Boston's Patrick Collins, born in Ireland, is elected to Congress.
	The Catholic newspaper *Republic* begins publication. (The newspaper continues until 1925.)
1883	City purchases the area that becomes Copley Square.
1884	Moon Island sewage treatment plant is completed at a cost of $6 million. The plant flushes sewage into Boston Harbor at high tide.
	Construction begins on Olmsted's Franklin Park.
(1890)	The *Chinese Monthly News* begins publication.
1892	Boston population reaches 448,000.
1893	The Metropolitan Park System is created to preserve parkland in the greater Boston area, including the Charles River, Revere Beach, Nantasket Beach, and the Blue Hills.
1894	Agudas Achem, the first Jewish temple in Roxbury, is built on Intervale Street.
1895	The Boston Public Library, Copley Square, opens.
1896	James Brendan Connelly of South Boston drops out of Harvard to compete in the first modern Olympics, winning the gold medal in the triple jump.
	Fannie Farmer publishes *The Boston Cooking-School Cookbook*.
1897	The first subway tunnel in the United States opens, connecting Park and Boylston Streets.
	The Boston Marathon is held for the first time.
1898	Northeastern University is founded.

A funeral on Harrison Avenue, 1890. By this time approximately two hundred Chinese immigrants lived in Boston's Chinatown.

1900s

1900	The Metropolitan Parks Commission presents a one-ton plaster topographic model of the park system at the Paris Exposition.
	Symphony Hall opens.
1901	King C. Gillette invents the "safety razor" in South Boston.
	The first St. Patrick's Day/Evacuation Day parade is held.
	Germania, a German-language newspaper, begins publication. (The newpaper continues until 1952.)
1902	*The Guardian*, William Monroe Trotter's paper, begins publication. (The newpaper continues until 1957.)
1903	Trotter is arrested for challenging Booker T. Washington at Columbus Avenue African Methodist Episcopal Church. Trotter and W. E. B. DuBois later found the National Association for Advancement of olored People (NAACP).
	The Boston Americans (later Red Sox) beat the Pittsburgh Pirates in the first World Series.

La *Gazetta*, Italian-language weekly, begins publication.
(The newspaper continues with some interruption until
1960; after 1975, it is published as the *Post Gazette*.)

1904 A subway tunnel under the harbor connects East Boston
with downtown.
The Wentworth Institute of Technology is founded.

1905 The *Jewish Advocate* begins publication.

1906 Suffolk University is founded.

1908 After a devastating Chelsea fire, many Jews move to the
West End or to Mattapan, in Dorchester.
The *Christian Science Monitor* begins publication.

1909 Edward Filene opens the "Automatic Bargain Basement"
in his Boston department store.
Boston population is 670,000.

1910 The Charles River Dam is completed.

1912 Fenway Park, home of the Boston Red Sox, opens.
The Red Sox defeat the New York Giants in the
World Series.
The Boston Fish Pier is built.
Hyde Park is annexed to the city.

*Filene's Basement,
founded in 1909*

1914 James Michael Curley is elected mayor for the first time.
The Boston Braves win the World Series.

1915 A tower is added to the Custom House, making it
the tallest building in Boston, at 496 feet.
The Red Sox win the World Series, defeating the
Philadelphia Phillies.

1916 *Haiyrenik*, an Armenian-language weekly, begins publication.
(The newspaper continues after 1939 as *Armenian Weekly*.)
The Red Sox defeat the Brooklyn Robins (later the Dodgers)
in the World Series.

1918 A flu epidemic kills thousands in September and
October. The Red Sox win the World Series, defeating
the Chicago Cubs, for their last world championship of
the twentieth century.
Jan Masaryk writes the Czechoslovakian Constitution at
the Czechoslovakian club on Columbia Road, South Boston.

1919 January 15: A molasses flood kills twenty-one in the
North End.
The Boston police go on strike.
Boston population reaches 750,000.

1920 Charles Ponzi bilks thousands of investors out of
millions of dollars.
Hebrew College is founded in Roxbury.

*Custom House Tower,
Boston's tallest building
until the era of sky-
scrapers began in the
1960s*

1921 The *Boston Post* wins a Pulitzer Prize for its investigation of the Ponzi story.

1922 James Michael Curley is elected to a second term as Boston mayor.

1924 WBZ radio station, from Springfield, moves to Boston.
John Cifrino's family builds the first supermarket in the country, at 600
Columbia Road, Dorchester.

1927	Langone funeral home in the North End is overwhelmed with mourners at the funerals of Bartolomeo Vanzetti and Nicola Sacco.
1929	The Boston Pops, under Arthur Fiedler, give the first concert on the Esplanade. Boston population reaches 780,000.
1930	James Michael Curley begins a third term as Boston's mayor.
1931	Horace Mann School for the Deaf opens in Roxbury.
1938	The Mary Ellen McCormack housing project is built.
1939	The Old Colony Housing Project opens in South Boston.
1941	Red Sox star Ted Williams bats .406, the last major league player to hit over .400. *Liria*, an Albanian-language weekly, begins publication.
1942	A fire at the Cocoanut Grove nightclub kills 492, making it the deadliest fire in the city's history.
1944	Richard Cushing becomes Archbishop of Boston.
1945	James Michael Curley is elected mayor for the final time.
1946	The Red Sox lose the World Series to the St. Louis Cardinals.
1947	The Metropolitan Transit Authority is established to oversee trolleys, subways, and elevated trains.
1948	Cleveland defeats the Boston Braves in the World Series.
1950	The Mystic River Bridge opens. Martin Luther King Jr. preaches at the Twelfth Baptist Church, Warren Street, Roxbury, while a theology student at Boston University. Boston population climbs to 801,000.
1951–1959	Construction of the Central Artery moves through downtown.
1951	The twenty-two-member city council, elected from wards, is replaced by a nine-member council chosen citywide.
1953	The Boston Braves leave for Milwaukee. The *Greek Sunday News* begins publication.
1954	Muhammad's Mosque 11 is opened in Dorchester by Malcolm X, formerly Malcolm Little of Roxbury.
1956	The Central Artery cuts a swath through Chinatown.
1957	The Boston Celtics win the first of their basketball championships.
1958–1965	The West End and Scollay Square are demolished in urban renewal projects.
1960	Boston population drops to 697,000.
1963	Parents in the South End organize a school boycott to protest inadequate conditions in their children's schools.
1965	A rematch of boxers Muhammad Ali and Sonny Liston, scheduled for the Boston Garden, is moved to Lewiston, Maine, after District Attorney Garrett Byrne proclaims the fight a "public nuisance." The *Bay State Banner*, a weekly for the African American community, begins publication.
1967	Mayor John Collins occupies the newly built City Hall at Government Center. Police remove protesting welfare mothers from welfare offices at Grove Hall, leading to two days of rioting. The Red Sox lose the World Series to the St. Louis Cardinals.

Bartolomeo Vanzetti (center) and Nicola Sacco (right) taken from jail to court, April 1927

Malcolm X, the charismatic leader of the Nation of Islam and the founder of Boston's first Nation of Islam mosque

1970	Boston population continues to drop to 641,000.
	The rock band Aerosmith begins performing in public.
1972	*Sampan*, a Chinese-language weekly, begins publication.
1973	Roxbury Community College is founded in Grove Hall.
1974	Charlestown Navy Yard closes.
1974–1976	Court-ordered busing, with the goal of desegregation, causes a crisis in Boston public schools..
1975	The Cincinnati Reds defeat the Red Sox in the World Series.
1976	Newly renovated Faneuil Hall Marketplace opens.
1978	*Semana*, a Spanish-language weekly, begins publication.
1980	Boston population declines to 563,000.
1981	The *Irish Echo* begins publication.
1983	Bay Windows, a gay community newspaper, begins publication.
1985	Federal Judge David Mazzone orders that Boston Harbor be cleaned up.
1986	The Boston Celtics win the NBA championship for the sixteenth time.
	The Boston Red Sox lose the World Series to the New York Mets.
1990	Thieves steal priceless works of art from the Isabella Stewart Gardner Museum. The paintings have not been recovered.
	Boston population is 575,000.
1991	Construction begins on the Big Dig project.
1993	Thomas M. Menino is elected mayor, the first non–Irish American mayor since 1929.
1995	The Ted Williams Tunnel opens.
(1997)	In a unanimous ruling, the U.S. Supreme Court finds that freedom of speech protects Allied War Veterans of South Boston in excluding groups with objectionable messages from the St. Patrick's Day parade.

St. Patrick's Day Parade, a watercolor by Dan McCole

2000s

2000	The Deer Island sewage treatment plant and its nine-mile outfall pipe are completed, as Boston Harbor begins to recover from centuries of pol-lution.
	For the first time, the U.S. Census shows that the white population of Boston is less than half of the total population of 589,000.
2001	John Joseph Moakley Courthouse is dedicated on Fan Pier.
2002	Scandal rocks the Roman Catholic Archdiocese of Boston, as Cardinal Bernard Law is discovered to have routinely reassigned clergy who had committed sexual crimes against children.
	Felix Arroyo is the first Hispanic to serve on the Boston City Council.
	Ted Williams dies at age eighty-three.
2003	Robert Travaglini of East Boston is elected president of the state senate.
	The new underground expressway opens, and demolition of the above-ground expressway begins.
	Sean O'Malley becomes the Archbishop of Boston and moves the archbishop's residence from Brighton to the South End.
2004	The Democratic National Convention is held in Boston.

further reading

OVERALL, THE INDISPENSABLE SOURCES are Josiah Quincy's *Municipal History of the Town and City of Boston, during Two Centuries 1630-1830* (1852); Justin Winsor's *Memorial History of Boston, 1630–1880* (1886); Walter Muir Whitehill and Lawrence Kennedy's *Boston: A Topographical History* (2000); Thomas H. O'Connor's *Bibles, Brahmins, and Bosses* (1991); Karl Haglund's *Inventing the Charles River* (2003); Nancy Seasholes's *Gaining Ground: A History of Land-Making in Boston* (2003); and Alex Kreiger and David Cobb's *Mapping Boston* (1999).

On the colonial period, see especially Edmund Morgan's *Puritan Dilemma: The Story of John Winthrop* (1958); Darrett B. Rutman's *Winthrop's Boston: A Portrait of a Puritan Town 1630–1649* (1965); Kenneth Silverman's *Life and Times of Cotton Mather* (1984); and Mark A. Peterson's *The Price of Redemption: The Spiritual Economy of Colonial New England* (1997).

On the American Revolution, see Richard Frothingham, *History of the Siege of Boston* (1903); Hiller B. Zobel, *The Boston Massacre* (1970); Alfred Young, *The Shoemaker and the Tea Party* (1999); David Hackett Fischer, *Paul Revere's Ride;* Bernard Bailyn, *The Ordeal of Thomas Hutchinson* (1974); Jayne Triber, *A True Republican: The Life of Paul Revere* (1998); Pauline Maier, *The Old Revolutionaries: Political Lives in the Age of Samuel Adams* (1980) and *From Resistance to Revolution: Colonial Radicals and the Development of American Opposition to Britain* (1974); and William Fowler's biography of John Hancock, *The Baron of Beacon Hill* (1980), and of Sam Adams, *Samuel Adams: Radical Puritan* (1997).

On Boston after the Revolution, see Robert Dalzell, *Enterprising Elite: The Boston Associates and the World They Made* (1987); Mathew H. Crocker, *The Magic of the Many: Josiah Quincy and the Rise of Mass Politics in Boston 1800–1830* (1999); Joseph McCarthy's edition of Bishop Benedict Fenwick's *Memoirs to Serve for the Future* (1978); Thomas H. O'Connor, *Boston Irish: A Political History* (1995) and *Boston Catholics: A History of the Church and Its People* (1998); James and Lois Horton, *Black Bostonians: Family Life and Community Struggle in the Antebellum North* (1999); Oscar Handlin, *Boston's Immigrants, 1790–1880: A Study in Acculturation* (1979 ed.); Elisabeth Gitter, *Imprisoned Guest: Samuel Howe and Laura Bridgman, the Original Deaf-Blind Girl* (2001) and Ernest Freeberg, *Education of Laura Bridgman: First Deaf-Blind Person to Learn Language* (2001); Thomas Brown, *Dorothea Dix: New England Reformer* (1998); Jonathan Messerli, *Horace Mann: A Biography* (1972); and Louise Hall Tharp, *Adventurous Alliance: The Story of the Agassiz Family of Boston* (1959).

On the Civil War, see Thomas O'Connor's *Civil War Boston: Home Front and Battlefield* (1997); Martin H. Blatt, Thomas J. Brown, and Donald Yacovone's *Hope & Glory: Essays on the Legacy of the Massachusetts Fifty-fourth* (2001); Henry Greenleaf Pearson's *The Life of John A. Andrew* (1904); Julia Ward Howe's *Memories of the Civil War* (1940); Christian Samito's *Commanding Boston's Irish Ninth: The Civil War Letters of Colonel Patrick R. Guiney* (1998); and Michael Macnamara's *The Irish Ninth in Bivouac and Battle* (1867).

On Boston since the Civil War, Louis P. Masur's *Autumn Glory: The First World Series* (2003) is about more than baseball. Leslie G. Ainley's *Boston Mahatma* (1949), on Martin Lomasney, Jack Beatty's *Rascal King: Life and Times of James Michael Curley* (1992), and Curley's own *I'd Do It Again* (1957) are good sources of information about Boston politics, though none of these books captures the politics as well as either Edwin O'Connor's novel *The Last Hurrah* (1956) or Charles Trout's *Boston, the Great Depression, and the New Deal* (1977).

On recent Boston history, see Gerald Gamm's *Urban Exodus: Why the Jews Left Boston and the Catholics Stayed* (1999); Thomas O'Connor's *Building a New Boston: Politics and Urban Renewal 1950–1970* (1993); David Kruh's *Always Something Doing: A History of Boston's Infamous Scollay Square* (1990); and Lawrence Vale's *From the Puritans to the Projects: Public Housing and Public Neighbors* (2000) and *Reclaiming Public Housing: A Half-Century of Struggle in Three Public Neighborhoods* (2002). J. Anthony Lukas's *Common Ground: A Turbulent Decade in the Lives of Three American Families* (1985) tells the story of three families during the busing years. Finally, the best political reports are by two insiders, Mel King's *Chain of Change: Struggles for Black Community Development* (1981) and *From Access to Power: Black Politics in Boston* (1986), and William M. Bulger's *While the Music Lasts: My Life in Politics* (1996).

acknowledgments

I AM ESPECIALLY INDEBTED to James Aloisi, Margot Balboni, Genie Beal, Margaret Carroll Bergman, Ellen Berkland, Alice Boelter, Marty Blatt, Eli Bortman, William M. Bulger, William M. Bulger Jr., Debby Cohen, Lawrence S. Di Cara, Dean Eastman, David I. Finnegan, William Fowler, Matthew and Susan Galbraith, Aram Goudsouzian, Sean Hennessey, Ann Hess, Greg Ketchen, Melvin H. King, Bob Krim, Henry Lachance, Vivien Li, William Martin, Louis P. Masur, Dan McCole, Joseph McEttrick, Ross Miller, Sherman "Pat" Morss Jr., Patric O'Brien, Dr. William J. Reid, Byron Rushing, Fred Salvucci, Paul Scali, Bill Shaevel, Chuck Turner, Jim Vrabel, Brian Wallace, Ted Widmer, and Hiller Zobel.

Thanks also to Aaron Schmidt of the Boston Public Library; Lorna Condon of the Society for the Preservation of New England Antiquities; Catharina Slautterback of the Boston Athenaeum; Nancy Richard and Ann Vosikas of the Bostonian Society; Peter Drummey and Anne Bentley of the Massachusetts Historical Society; John McColgan and Kristen Swett at the City of Boston Archives; Michael Comeau of the Massachusetts Archives; Tamsen George at the Shirley-Eustis House; Susan Greendyke Lachevre at the Massachusetts Art Commission; Margaret Gonsalves at the Archives of the Archdiocese of Boston; Julia Collins at the Moakley Archives, Suffolk University; and Michael Quinlin of the Boston Irish Tourism Association.

Webster Bull at Commonwealth Editions suggested the project; Liz Nelson and Penny Stratton kept it focused. At Suffolk I am indebted to colleagues Kenneth S. Greenberg, Robert Bellinger, Bob Dugan, Joseph McCarthy, James Nelson, and Da Zheng, and my students in History 383, "Boston: Heritage of a City" through whose eyes I continue to see Boston anew. No thanks are enough for my wife Phyllis; and for our sons, John Robert and Philip, I only can hope this book will help them better understand their hometown.

index

Page numbers in italics refer to illustrations. Material in the chronology (pages 112–119) is not included in the index.

Illustration Credits

COVER ILLUSTRATIONS Front cover: "Southeast View of the Great Town of Boston" (1700s), courtesy of the Bostonian Society/Old State House. Back cover, clockwise from top left: Boston massacre, courtesy of the Commonwealth of Massachusetts, Archives; Sgt. William Carney, courtesy of the Massachusetts Historical Society; immigrants approaching Boston, courtesy of the Boston Public Library; Beacon Hill under excavation, courtesy of the Bostonian Society/Old State House; Samuel Adams, courtesy of the Museum of Fine Arts; John F. Kennedy and others, photo by John Tlumacki, courtesy of the *Boston Globe;* urban renewal, courtesy of the Boston Public Library; Fort Warren, courtesy of the Boston Athenaeum; Trimount, courtesy of the Bostonian Society/Old State House; Anne Hutchinson statue, courtesy of the Boston Public Library; John Winthrop, courtesy of the Massachusetts Art Commission; Johnny Kelley, photo by Leslie Jones, courtesy of the Boston Public Library. Author photo on back cover by Jeffry Pike, Harvard University, Division of Continuing Education.

TEXT ILLUSTRATIONS Page 2 (facing title page): Carleton's map of Boston, 1775, courtesy of the Bostonian Society/Old State House. Title page and page 6: "Southeast View of the Great Town of Boston" (1700s), courtesy of the Bostonian Society/Old State House. Copyright page: Chinese dragon dance, 1929, and Custom House tower, photo by Leslie Jones, courtesy of Boston Public Library; Tercentenary Monument, photo by Ross Miller, courtesy of Mr. Miller. Pages 9, 15, 18, 22 (right), 27, 33, 35, 38, 42, 44, 52 (top), 61 (right), 65, 69, 70, 71 (top), 74 (top), 75 (bottom), 78, 97 (photo by John Harper), 113, courtesy of the Bostonian Society/Old State House; pages 10, 13, photo by Ross Miller, courtesy of Mr. Miller; pages 11, 19 (bottom), 34, 39, 49 (middle and bottom), 55, 58, 59, 62, 66 (right), 67 (left), 71 (bottom), 99 (right), 114, 115, courtesy of the Boston Athenaeum; page 12, courtesy of the Massachusetts Art Commission; pages 16 (photo by Ernest Hill), 17, 22 (left), 49 (top), 52 (bottom), 53 (top), 54 (from *Ballou's Pictorial),* 56 (top and bottom), 67 (right), 72, 73 (bottom), 74 (bottom), 75 (top), 77, 79, 80, 81, 83, 84, 85, 86 (photo by Grace Line), 87, 88, 89 (top and bottom), 90, 92 (left and right, photo by Leslie Jones), 93 (top left photo by E. E. Bond; others by Leslie Jones), 98 (left), 101 (top and bottom), 103, 107 (photo by Ollie Noonan, *Boston Herald-Traveler*), 116, 117 (bottom, photo by Leslie Jones), 118 (top, photo by Leslie Jones), 118 (bottom, photo by George Dixon, *Boston Herald-Traveler,* July 1962), courtesy of the Boston Public Library; page 19 (top), from *New England Magazine,* 1901, courtesy of Ruth Owen Jones; pages 24, 25, 40 (top), 45, 57, courtesy of Sawyer Library, Suffolk University; pages 100, 117 (top), courtesy of Suffolk University Archives; pages 104, 110, courtesy of the John Joseph Moakley Archives, Suffolk University; pages 26, 32, 66 (left), courtesy of the Massachusetts Historical Society; page 29, courtesy of the Museum of Fine Arts; page 31, courtesy of the Commonwealth of Massachusetts, Archives; pages 36, 37, courtesy of the Shirley-Eustis House; pages 40 (bottom), 73 (top), 119, paintings by Dan McCole, courtesy of Mr. McCole; pages 43, 109, photos by Sherman "Pat" Morss, courtesy of Mr. Morss; pages 46, 51, 60, 61 (left), courtesy of the Library of Congress; page 47, painting by Henry A. Lachance, courtesy of Mr. Lachance; page 48, courtesy of Concord Free Library; page 53 (bottom left and right), courtesy of Archives, Roman Catholic Archdiocese of Boston; page 64, courtesy of Michael P. Quinlin, Boston Irish Tourism Association; page 76, courtesy of William M. Bulger; page 82 (top and bottom), courtesy of National Park Service, Frederick Law Olmsted National Historic Site; page 95, photo by Margot Balboni, courtesy of Ms. Balboni; page 96, photo by John Tlumacki, courtesy of the *Boston Globe;* pages 98–99, photo by Irene Schwachman, courtesy of the Boston Athenaeum; page 102, courtesy of Mel King; page 106, courtesy of Fred Salvucci; page 111, courtesy of the Massachusetts Water Resource Authority.